What people ar

NOTOR.⌣⌣

"Through heartfelt honesty and incredible clarity of vision, Doug Garasic takes the reader on a journey of discovery and reflection. This book so eloquently dives into the heart of the gospel, and the compassion that Jesus showed the world. There is so much more to life than superficial concerns and competition; there is the pure joy of lifting up others through the words of Jesus Christ. I believe *Notorious* has the power to change so many lives and inspire the church to reach even greater heights."

PASTOR MATTHEW BARNETT
SENIOR PASTOR OF ANGELUS TEMPLE AND CO-FOUNDER OF THE DREAM CENTER

"Doug Garasic is funny and a solid young leader worth learning from. I'm glad to call him a friend. You will love reading this book. I am a big fan of authenticity, and he definitely aced it in *Notorious*."

RICK BEZET
PASTOR OF NEW LIFE CHURCH IN ARKANSAS AND AUTHOR OF *BE REAL: BECAUSE FAKE IS EXHAUSTING*

"The always unconventional and out of the box Doug Garasic has now, through his book, *Notorious*, given the framework for everyone who would dare to embrace the radical message of the Gospel."

BISHOP MICHAEL S. PITTS
PASTOR OF CORNERSTONE CHURCH AND OVERSEER OF CORNERSTONE GLOBAL NETWORK

"I was originally rooting for this book to be titled *Garasic Park* (perfect title, right?). Now that I've actually read it, I'm just plain rooting for Doug Garasic. God is doing something mighty through Doug's ministry in northeast Ohio. *Notorious* will give you a taste."

JONATHAN HERRON
AUTHOR OF *COMEDY-DRIVEN LEADERSHIP* AND PASTOR OF LIFE CHURCH MICHIGAN

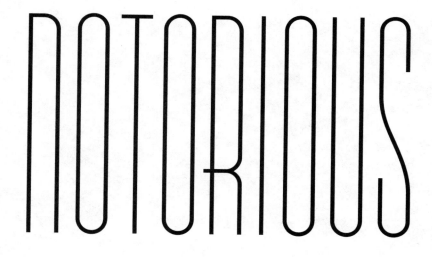

NOTORIOUS

THE GOSPEL JESUS INTENDED

Jennifer Perez

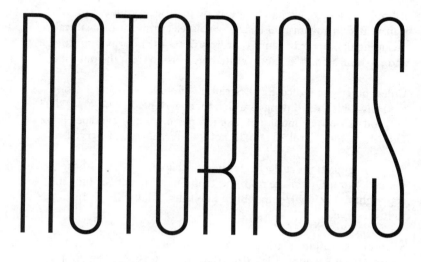

NOTORIOUS

THE GOSPEL JESUS INTENDED

DOUGLAS J. GARASIC

KOPI
BOOKS

NOTORIOUS
Published by Kopi Books
105B 5555 Youngstown Warren Road
Niles, OH 44446 U.S.A.

ISBN 978-0-578-14983-7

The Team: Stephanie Garasic, Andrew Heller, Mary Bell
Cover Design: Isaac Weisman

Printed in the United States of America
First Edition 2014

To every person who has been screwed up by religion, or was taught to believe a gospel that was not even close to the heart of God, this book is for you.

CONTENTS

FOREWORD

The first time I met Doug was on a phone call. A mutual friend suggested that we connect, and Doug reached out. He talked blindingly fast. I'm from Texas; Doug is from Ohio. I needed a translator. It was a hilarious and explosive blend of ideas and pop culture references, which Doug is famous for. Doug's passion for people was immediately evident. I thought, "Here's a guy who is changing the world and also may need some sort of medication." He was not only sharing ideas, he was also reaching for knowledge. Through the course of our conversation, he kept asking questions. There was this raw desire to know stuff. Not just random information – Doug was on a quest to discover methods, processes, and secrets that push people to the next level. As you will see, his book is filled with them.

He scheduled me to come and speak at The Movement

Conference, a power packed two-day conference that his church hosts every year. I had no idea that the church, the conference, and Doug's friendship would ultimately bless me more than I was blessing them.

It was my trip to The Movement in Ohio that helped me see what God had up his divine sleeve for my own future. I was blown away by their innovation and deep commitment to reaching the city. I don't know that I've ever met anyone more committed to fulfilling their calling than Doug and Stephanie Garasic. They gave up everything to invest their lives into planting a church and wouldn't accept the words "quit" or "can't."

When I visited The Movement, their Niles Campus was one year old, and they were already in the process of planting another campus. How that second campus unfolded was amazing. I was able to walk through the building during the remodeling process. It was an old bar. Not just a regular old bar, but a seriously dangerous menace-to-the-neighborhood old bar. In fact, there had been a murder on the doorstep of the bar just months before. That's what brought the property to Doug's attention. When The Movement purchased the property, the building's owner hung a huge sign on the outside brick wall that read, "Change is coming. Thank God."

Seeing this radical drive to accomplish God's purpose for the Kingdom turned a crank on the inside of me. I was at a particularly challenging time in my life, and Doug's faith was contagious. His unquenchable belief that God will not let you down if you trust him for the impossible inspired me. It inspired me to see the impossible differently.

Since The Movement launched in 2012, God has blessed them in a tremendous way. More than 500 excited people showed up for the opening of their first campus, and since then the church has exploded with growth. In two years, more than 780 people have given their lives to Jesus, and one night last summer they baptized 200 people in a middle of the mall parking lot. They aren't slowing down either. In addition to starting Neo Academy to equip leaders for ministry, they are also launching their third campus in early 2015.

Spreading the unstoppable love of Jesus is at the core of everything they do. Doug took me to a sandwich shop after we toured the bar-soon-to-be-church. When we walked to the counter, they knew him. They liked him. This is not always the case with pastors, but Doug told me he had encouraged his entire staff and volunteers to patronize the sandwich place in an effort to spread the love of Jesus. It was in this moment I realized that Doug understood the difference between his calling and his gifting.

I've met too many empty preachers who love to preach but don't love people. Somehow they forgot that their calling is people and their gifting is preaching. If you get these two confused, you'll prostitute your calling for your gift; you'll go wherever your gift is honored whether you are called there or not. Chances are, if you are constantly moving away from people, you aren't following Jesus. Doug is called to people. He is the same whether he is in the pulpit or, as you'll find out in a few pages, at a bar hearing a friend's band. This is why The Movement is reaching lost people with the life-altering Gospel of Jesus.

Doug and Stephanie also have a heart for church planters. They understand the sheer terror of leaving everything that you've ever known and banking the farm on a church plant that may or may not work. They take the time to call, encourage, laugh with and lead other leaders.

And now, a book.

The journey that Doug will take you on is going to rock your world, crack you up and change your life. Just prepare yourself. When I first read this book I was at my desk in the middle of a super busy work day and thought I would just skim a couple of paragraphs and save the rest for later. Four chapters deep, I was forced to put it down because I was late for an appointment.

Doug's relentless pursuit of God's heart challenged me, and I know that it will challenge you as well. Immerse yourself in this book. Read it with a highlighter in hand. There will be moments of self-discovery and many more moments of God-discovery. I actually paused in several chapters to send encouraging texts to those that I felt compassion for and sent up a few prayers of thanks for those who have had compassion on me. This book will drive you to recognize your own inadequacies, but also encourage you to embrace your true identity: Your God identity.

Very few people capture the raw grace of the gospel like Doug. This book is written like a blue-collar handbook, but referenced like a theological textbook. It will drive you to change and that's exactly the goal of the gospel. As you read Doug's anecdotes and advice, don't hide who you really are – embrace it and let God change you. He loves you. He's calling you. Now he wants to blow your mind. Let him.

– JEREMY FOSTER
PASTOR OF HOPE CITY HOUSTON

PROLOGUE

First, I want to say how absolutely pumped and honored I am that you have invested some cash and time into this book. I never envisioned myself as a writer (nor did any of my English teachers – how do you like me now, Mr. Kozar?!), but about two years ago I was preparing to preach for my little church plant in Ohio and came across the scripture we are going to unpack over the following chapters. Like most church planters who are far too busy and have far too little help, I was rushing to prepare a series I was teaching called "A Simple Story." In this series, we were diving into the stories, or parables, that Jesus told. When I read Jesus' words in Luke 15, my initial response was, "Cool, Jesus wants us to leave the ninety-nine and go after the one; that makes sense. We all need to love and care for those around us. It's almost too simple."

As several months passed, I moved on to new preaching material and became consumed by the many tasks of a growing church: connecting with new people, managing budgets, recruiting volunteers, setting up and tearing down every weekend, and keeping my wife from stabbing me in the eye because ministry can be very demanding. But in my rare moments alone, that scripture just wouldn't leave my mind. I found myself going back to it during my quiet time, rereading it, thinking about it, and even bringing it up randomly in meetings and times of preaching different subjects. I'm not a guy who's "super-spiritual" about everything – God usually has to hit me over the head with a bag of nickels to get my attention – but this passage of scripture was really getting to me.

About a year later, I was on vacation with my wife and some friends in sunny Key West. When I go on vacation I like to get up early, grab my Bible, and head out to the deck to read while I listen to the ocean and think, "Why doesn't Lake Erie look like this?" (That's an inside joke for the northern folk.) One such morning, I was sitting with an open Bible, hoping that the wind would begin to flip the pages and land on exactly what God wanted me to read. Instead, I found myself back at the same familiar spot in Luke 15. But then the strangest thing happened. This one oddly placed word jumped off the page at me. When I saw this word I immediately felt that God-sized bag of nickels getting ready to smack me over the head! Since then, I have researched and discovered that this word appears in very few translations of this passage, but it was there in my dark blue, seam-tattered, 1st edition TruthQuest Bible (New Living Translation) that was given to me by one of my mentors.

Did you ever have the feeling that you stumbled onto something big? Not just oh-that's-cool-let-me-hashtag-it big, but something that will alter the way you think, the decisions you make, and ultimately the reason for your existence? I just had – all because of one little word God placed on a page.

It's funny how one word from God can do more than a thousand self-help books (even this one). God had given me an invitation to think differently. Not that my previous way of thinking was wrong, I mean, I loved God and pastored a church and did my best to love people. But sometimes just because something isn't wrong, doesn't make it right. I often say that good is the enemy of great. I believe God has something better than what we choose to settle for. We can get so easily consumed by doing the "right" things that we miss the point, but all it takes is one word from God to redirect us. I stumbled on this one passage (Luke 15) and caught this one line (verse one) and discovered this one word (if you don't know what the word is, close the book and look at the title) that totally changed my life. If you are willing to go on this journey with me, it might change your life, too.

Disclaimer: Some of what you read on the following pages might upset or even offend you. My intention is not to offend for its own sake, but to wake you up to the gospel that Jesus intended. The gospel that Jesus preached and lived, the gospel for which he died, looks very different from the one that many of us who have been claiming to follow Jesus are preaching and living. Something needs to change ... and it's not Jesus.

In this book, I am going to challenge you to get out of your comfort zone. I am going to challenge you to stop caring about your reputation. I am going to invite you to live free from status quo Christianity. And I am willing to bet that as we go deeper down this rabbit hole you're going to encounter the truth of the gospel – this good news, this great story – in a way that will rearrange your priorities and wreck your life. With one word, God might speak to you to love people you don't even like, or to look beyond lifestyles to reach someone to whom you normally wouldn't be caught talking. With one word, God might capture your wandering heart and change the way you've been thinking about yourself and him for so many years. With one word, God created the heavens and the earth, so why shouldn't we expect that this one word will transform our lives?

It's time to let go of our previous way of thinking and discover the gospel Jesus intended.

CHAPTER ONE

NOTORIOUS

NO·TO·RI·OUS

"FAMOUS OR WELL KNOWN
typically for some bad quality or deed;
WIDELY KNOWN FOR A BAD
OR UNFAVORABLE QUALITY"

In 1925, mobsters ran the streets in cities across America. During Prohibition, when moving drugs and alcohol was one of the most lucrative occupations around, one up-and-comer, a 26-year-old kid, began running the streets of Chicago. He came from a well-respected Italian family but got tangled up with shady characters at a very young age. Soon he was well known for running prostitution rings, organizing bootleggers, and violently killing anyone who got in his way.

From the time he came on the scene, this mobster flipped not only the city of Chicago but the entire United States upside down with the atrocities his gang, the Chicago Outfit, committed. Everyone knew that when the man with the scar on his face walked into a room, they needed to stop talking and start listening to exactly what he had to say. His reputation and influence extended his control not only to crime circles, but to the government as well. After the Saint Valentine's Day massacre in 1929, the desire to put this man behind bars became priority number one for every law enforcement department around the city.

In 1931, this mafia boss was arrested for tax evasion and was indicted for owing the government more than $200,000. But before his death in 1947 and for decades after, he was heralded as one of the most savage, most intelligent, most feared, most notorious gangster of all time. Who was he?

Al Capone. Scarface.

Even though he's been dead for more than half a century, we still know his name. We've seen movies based on his life. Instead of describing his career, I could have probably written "say hello to my little friend" and you would have thought of his nickname (from the 1983 film, *Scarface*). He's been the model for almost every single portrayal of mafia bosses for the last eighty years. Why? Because Al Capone is the most infamous gangster known to the world. He's notorious.

———————

In my own younger years, I, too, became well known for causing trouble. Don't worry, I didn't come anywhere close to wreaking the kind of havoc we've just been discussing. Most of my pranks were harmless and merely disruptive, but I realized very young that I liked attention, and that the best way to get everyone's attention was by speaking out of turn, making people laugh, acting like a fool, or doing something stupid. I usually got caught, which only served to spread my reputation as a troublemaker more widely among my peers, parents, principals, and even some of the "po-po" (aka police) in my small town (I was never arrested, just got picked up a few times). By the time I was in junior high, my mom's first question whenever the school called was, "What did Doug do now?"

One of the highlights of my seventh grade year was my bus driver, Pat. She was fun and easy to talk to. Even though she only came in at about five feet tall on a good day, she knew how to handle herself with a bunch of hormone-crazed middle schoolers. I respected Pat, probably because she really didn't care much how we acted up while on the bus. One morning as I waited outside for the school bus, I knew something was wrong. The bus was ten minutes late, and the bus was always late when there was a substitute bus driver. If Pat was out sick, this was not good news for me. Sure enough, when I boarded the bus, I was greeted by a substitute bus driver who looked like she meant business.

At that moment, I had a choice to make: I could continue my legacy as comedian, entertainer, and instigator of foolishness, or I could take a break from my antics for one morning, since it was much more likely I'd get in trouble with the substitute driver. I chose the second option, dropped into my seat near the back of the bus (In the world of school bus hierarchy, the ruler of the bus sat in the back. I was in seat #28 of 32 – so close!), and leaned my head against the window. As the vibrations slowly shook my brain into unconsciousness, an unfortunate situation began to play out around me. Some girls in the next seat started throwing paper wads at the "not cool kids" towards the front of the bus. Of course, the "not cool kids" retaliated with their own paper wads, and the barrage quickly escalated from paper to pens to notebooks and other various school supplies flying back and forth over my head.

Just as I became aware of the battle raging around me, I noticed the girl in the seat next to me reach into the front pocket of her backpack like she was unsheathing an ancient sword. She might as well have been doing just that, because what she pulled out had the makings of the perfect weapon. It was a massive Cadillac emblem made of solid metal. This thing must have weighed four or five pounds. I had no idea where she would have obtained this object, but as she revealed her weapon of choice to me, she informed me that she was going to chuck this metal emblem of destruction at the girls in the front of the bus to teach them a lesson.

Now I was paying attention. Something told me this could only end badly. The girl reared back and catapulted the Cadillac emblem as hard as she could into the front of the bus, with rage like a drunken Cleveland Browns fan throwing glass bottles onto the football field (random fact: this actually happened at a Cleveland Browns vs. Jacksonville Jaguars game in December 2001, and it was the last time glass bottles were allowed in any NFL stadium). Unfortunately, her aim was about as accurate as a drunken Browns fan, and she missed her mark. The emblem flew past her intended targets, whizzed past the substitute bus driver's ear, and smashed into the windshield. The window cracked, the substitute panicked, the bus started swerving, and the middle schoolers began screaming like they were back in preschool.

As you can imagine, the substitute was absolutely fuming. She instantly got on her walkie talkie and relayed what had happened to the bus garage. When we arrived at the school and the substitute parked the bus, we all stood up to get off the bus like nothing had happened, but, shaking with anger, the substitute immediately told us to sit back down. We sat and waited for what seemed like hours as the principal marched down from the school building and climbed the stairs onto the now silent bus. With a beet-red face, the principal began laying into the entire bus and letting us know that we all could have died because of our stupidity. At the end of his rant, I specifically remember him saying, "I want to know who threw the Cadillac emblem!"

For once in my life I was sitting calmly in the back of the bus with my unorganized Trapper Keeper, feeling confident that I actually made a positive decision not to be involved in the shenanigans that had just taken place. Obviously, no one on the bus spoke up, because where I come from "snitches get stitches" (bad joke, but you're going to get a lot more of those, so please brace yourself). So the principal turned to the substitute bus driver and asked her who she thought the culprit was. I will never forget her response. She looked in her oversized rearview mirror and said, "All I can remember is seeing the redhead."

If you have never seen me, yes, I am a ginger.

Instantly, I had that sick feeling in the pit of my stomach. The principal responded, "I knew Garasic must have had something to do with it! Get off this bus, young man, and get into my office!" I was dumbfounded that I was the one being blamed for this offense. They threatened that I would have to pay for the shattered windshield, but instead I was simply suspended from the bus for several days, and the Great Bus Windshield Cracking was added to my rap sheet. No matter how much I tried to explain that I had nothing to do with the situation, no one believed me.

I was notorious.

Because I had been caught in similar foolish situations so many times in my past, I was pointed out as the guilty party, even when I was innocent. It was widely known that "the redhead" was a proven troublemaker, officially labeled as a "disturber of the peace," like Gandalf in *The Lord of the Rings* (not only will I tell lots of bad jokes, but I'll also get my nerd on occasionally), and I realized then that there was not much I could do to change that. No matter how I chose to act, my reputation preceded me.

This is why, years later, when I read the words "notorious sinner" in Luke 15, they struck me in a powerful way.

Now, when I was young I didn't realize the negative connotations that the word notorious carried. I just wanted to be well-known, and it didn't matter to me what I was known for. I think we all have some innate desire to be recognized, to be known. We want to be famous, and if that seems unattainable, many will aim for being infamous instead. Some people work hard to maintain a good reputation, and others delight in the fact that they are good at being bad.

When someone is labeled as notorious, they don't need an introduction; their reputation precedes them everywhere they go. From a rambunctious kid like me, always getting in trouble, to someone like Al Capone, the most notorious gangster in history – the Bible says these are the types of people who were often hanging around Jesus.

I identified with people who were labeled "bad" – those no one ever expected to do anything good – because that's who I was. Perhaps you're reading this, thinking, "Okay that's fine for you, but I haven't committed any major crimes; I'm a good person!"

Are you?

I'm not casting any judgment. I've already revealed my own flawed character to you. But let's get honest for a minute. Just because no one else knows about your issues doesn't mean they aren't there. We all seem to have that one thing that we just can't get past. That thing that eats at us and ultimately defines us. The mother who is wracked with guilt and takes it out on her kids. The pastor who is secretly addicted to porn. The high school student who has given into peer pressure one too many times. The grandma who had an abortion forty years ago. The man, consumed with greed, who is constantly chasing success. Whatever your age, race, gender, or status, you have it. Fill in the blank. And you know if it ever got out, that is how you'd be known for the rest of your life. You'd be notorious.

But guess what? You already are. The Bible says every single one of us have sinned and fallen short of God's standard.[1] God knows all of your struggles, all of your weaknesses, your failures, your sins – whether anyone else does or not.

Many of the crowd who followed Jesus were known for ungodly things, but they chose to take audience with the godly and did not feel ashamed. There is something about Jesus that makes even the worst sinners feel comfortable around him. Yet so many of us waste time trying to get our lives cleaned up before pursuing a relationship with Jesus, thinking God can't use us because of our pasts. We try to keep him at a distance so our deep, dark secrets can stay hidden. But consider this: It's only those who think they're righteous that feel uncomfortable around Jesus.

It's okay to admit you're not okay. The good news is that Jesus intended to pursue people just like you and me. The scripture and story that we are going to discuss throughout this book is what Jesus wants you to know about why he came to this earth, and what he expects from you ... and it's not what you might think.

REFLECTION & APPLICATION

What are you known for? What makes you notorious?

What do you want to be known for?

Read Proverbs 22.
Based on this passage, what are some habits you need to adopt to begin to reshape your notoriety?

CHAPTER TWO

THE GOSPEL OF COMPASSION

> **"WHEN HE SAW THE CROWDS, HE HAD COMPASSION FOR THEM,** *because they were harrassed & helpless* **LIKE SHEEP WITH OUT A SHEPHERD"**
>
> *Matthew 9:36, NIV*

I was 18 years old when I became a follower of Christ. Before that, loving people was very hard for me. I didn't forgive easily; I only really cared about myself. I grew up knowing enough about God to go to a Christian preschool (where I'm told I once locked another kid in the bathroom) and to attend church on Christmas and Easter, but I never really understood it until later. As you already know, I was a difficult child and an even more unruly teenager. By the time I reached the end of my junior year, I had been suspended so many times that returning to my public high school was not an option. I had made a mess of my life and found myself in a situation where the only way I could graduate from high school on time was to finish my senior year at a private Christian school.

I was totally out of my element at this school. There were a total of five students in my class (you didn't misread that: five!). I had to wear white button-down shirts, black tie, the whole nine yards. One time, they tried to paddle me as a punishment; I was an 18 year old senior – that was NOT happening. It was very much what you would think when it comes to strict fundamentalist ideals. Definitely not my style, but I was willing to do whatever was necessary to get that diploma, and this was my only option. Between uniforms and policies, I was exposed to many uncomfortable situations that I didn't understand, and much less enjoyed, but also for the first time in my life, I was exposed to the Gospel of Jesus in a way that actually made sense to me.

Let me explain.

Every week we would have to attend chapel with a different preacher or speaker who would show up in a suit and tie, ready to preach the Word to all of the students and try to get them "saved" for the hundredth time. But one week a guy showed up to speak in an Abercrombie t-shirt (I was in high school before the hipster era, when wearing Abercrombie meant you had rich, prep style, which I pretended was my style), with his tattoo showing. I remember thinking, "Dude must have paid some serious cash for that shirt," and I couldn't believe he had a tattoo just like I did, which wasn't really acceptable at a Christian school (in the early 2000's, tattoos were still taboo in churches, unlike today when people think you are weird if you don't have a tattoo). Bottom line: This guy was different from any Christian I had seen.

Because I could relate to him, Andy Warren spoke into my life in a way that no one else could up to that point. His message wasn't condescending or over my head. He didn't stand up there and read scripture after scripture that I could not understand, like some of the other pastors I had heard. What he said actually made sense, and I was intrigued. After Andy spoke at the chapel that day, I wanted to hear more of what he had to say. I started attending his youth ministry, at first because there was a girl there that I liked, but then because it was unlike anything else I had experienced in a church. There was loud music, lights, smoke, and kids that didn't fit my stereotype of "church kids" – you know, the ones who sit in a cinderblock room on steel chairs, eating animal crackers and staring at each other in their circle of awkwardness. These were athletes, cheerleaders, and "normal" kids like I wanted to be. Pastor Andy – muscular, tattooed, with a crazy personality – was the first Christian man that I could see myself wanting to be like. For the first time, I entertained the thought that this Jesus thing might actually be something for my life.

After I had attended youth ministry for about six weeks, Andy preached a message about salvation. He explained that if we had never truly confessed our sin to God and asked God to forgive us, then Jesus was not in our hearts. He made it clear that even though Jesus, or the idea of Jesus, may have been in our minds he needed to be invited into our hearts and lives. I remember Andy saying, "If you want to accept Christ, this is your time." Andy asked for every person to close their eyes and bow their heads, and said that whoever wanted to give their hearts to Jesus should come up to the front.

My heart was racing, my hands were sweating. I knew that I needed Jesus because I was so sick of living my life without him. As I stood up and began to walk toward the front of the room, I realized two things: One, I was the only person walking to the front, and, two, everyone was staring at me. Remember, I didn't grow up in church so I had no idea that few people listened when someone said "bow your heads and close your eyes." Things got real very quickly. A million thoughts raced through my mind about what people would think of me now, but I gritted my teeth and kept going. I had no idea what to do when I reached the front of the room, so I just knelt down in the fetal position. In a moment I noticed someone kneeling beside me and opened my eyes to see big alligator tears splash on the ground. Pastor Andy was there and he prayed with me, as I asked Jesus to forgive me for all my sins and come into my life.

That night was a pivotal moment for me, but I quickly realized that just because I had asked Jesus into my heart didn't mean that all of my issues, problems, and personality deficiencies magically disappeared. I had spent the first 18 years of my life as a notorious sinner, and it was going to take more than an 18-second prayer to detoxify from that lifestyle. No one who had known me during that time ever expected me to change.

I had a lot of issues – anger, lust, selfishness (to name a few) – and I had to learn how to deal with them. All of my desires centered around pleasing myself, and I still had this knack of causing trouble and mischief in almost every situation. I needed to be retaught how to be a human being, and on top of that, how to be a Christ-following human being. On my own, I would have never been able to clean up the mess of my life, but I had the Great Counselor[1] with me and inside of me to take me through this painstaking process of dealing with my junk.

Most of us love to throw our junk in the closet and forget about it, but God really wants us to sort it out. Some things we find might just need cleaning off or repairing, but some we need to throw out. If we will let him, God will bring us through a process of healing and correction and growth, purging and reforming us so that we will be more like Jesus. It's a difficult journey to walk, and it will continue throughout your entire life, but it is worth it.

I walked though this process for about a year within Pastor Andy's youth ministry. I was fully committed. If you ever see me get into a swimming pool (which is about once every seven years, because this ginger skin doesn't do well in the sun), you would not see me checking the water with my toe and slowly inching my way into the water; I just dive right in. I did the same thing when I found Jesus. Even though I was still pretty much a heathen, I dove into the leadership of youth ministry and took every opportunity to grow and learn from Pastor Andy, who seemed like the only person who believed in me.

When I graduated high school, I became an adult leader for the youth, and found myself constantly disappointing Andy and the team who led the youth ministry. I made a fool of myself at seemingly every turn. I was wildfire – uncontrollable and often destructive, but passionate. I was taught, and I believe this with all my heart, that God would rather have wildfire than no fire at all. When you have wildfire, you can learn to contain it, direct it and use it for strength; but if you have no fire, you are left out in the cold. Believe me, I was the definition of wildfire, and I needed constant direction on how to harness my passion.

So, when Andy left the youth ministry to pastor another church, I followed him there as an intern. I had no one else in my life at that time to teach me, so I moved into his spare room and began trying to learn how to do what he did. During this time, even though I didn't realize it, other people were noticing that I was finally starting to "get it." I was renewing my mind (like it says in Romans 12), changing my behaviors, and, because of those obvious changes, I was becoming a person who could be trusted a little bit (key word being little).

One evening after dinner with Andy and his family, I was helping his wife Beth clean up the kitchen and chatting with her about how far I had come. Beth is as nice as nice can be, but she's also very honest and won't hesitate to speak the truth with a smile. So when she stopped and turned to me in the kitchen, she said, "Doug, can I tell you my first opinion of you? Can I tell you what I told my husband? I used to get so upset at Andy for giving you chance after chance after chance. I would ask him why he gave you so many opportunities when all you ever did was drop the ball every time."

Ouch. There was that sick feeling in the pit of my stomach, just like on the bus in seventh grade. I had no idea why Andy kept giving me all those chances either, because I certainly knew I didn't deserve it. But Beth continued, "Andy's response to me really changed my perspective. He said, 'Beth, I know Doug fails a lot. I know he drops the ball. But if I am not there for him now, then the Devil will pull him right back into the life that Jesus has saved him from.'"

38

In that moment, as a 19-year-old kid, my perspective changed too. I knew that I caused people trouble, but I never knew that there were people who were questioning Andy's leadership because of me. Why was Andy willing to risk his reputation, even his ministry, for my sake?

Compassion.

Andy had compassion for me because he had been where I was. He hadn't grown up as a Christian, and had to go through a difficult journey before he really started to follow God. As I think about my life, the reason I am who I am today has a lot to do with Andy's compassion for me. He could have had a much easier, more comfortable life and ministry if he hadn't taken me under his wing, but he wanted to see God change my life in the same way that God had changed his life.

The dictionary definition of compassion is "pity or concern for the suffering of others."[2] My definition of compassion is this:

Compassion = Come / Past / Something

When we have come past a difficult situation, horrible tragedy, empty life, perpetual struggle, bad reputation, or whatever it may be, we should be able to identify with others who are currently experiencing those same challenges. Too often we forget how screwed up we were before we knew Jesus, and we are unwilling to have compassion for others. If we fail to realize we are nothing and can do nothing without God, then every time someone screws up around us, we will judge and think, "Why don't they just fix themselves?"

But they can't, just like we couldn't. Only God can fix and save and change us. It's time for us to open our minds and our hearts and start loving people right where they are. God loved us while we were still sinners.[3] Compassion drove Jesus' ministry while he was on earth, and it should drive us as well.

————————

I've come past a lot of things in my life, and that has shaped me and my ministry into what it is today. When I first planted my church in northeast Ohio, I realized that everywhere I went in our community was a mission field of people who needed Jesus. Statistics tell us that in some places 8 out of 10 people in their twenties or younger do not actively attend a church or follow Christ. This number is growing every day, so my goal is to go after anyone God places in front of me. I believe it is foolish to pray "God send me someone that you want me to reach." What we should be praying is "God show me how to speak to the people I see every single day. Show me how to live in a way that makes them want to know You."

If we begin to pray this type of prayer, we will position ourselves so that whenever we cross paths with someone, we will be ready to love them like Jesus does. I think the apostle Paul said it best, "I have become all things to all people so that by all possible means I might save some."[4] I have worked to model my life after this principle. Every day I try to find someone to impact and love. Living this way doesn't allow me to have bad days. Even though the circumstances and situations around me may be difficult and testing, I choose whether or not I'm going to let them affect my daily mission.

On one typical cloudy day in northeast Ohio, I was driving by the local Starbucks and I noticed Phil, who attended my church and had recently started following Christ, standing outside talking to a girl I didn't know. Phil saw me and flagged me down. I stopped my car (and traffic) to say hi, as Phil introduced me as his pastor to his friend Lindsay. She was wearing a Starbucks apron, which caught my attention because I had been specifically praying that we as a church could reach out to people who worked at this very Starbucks. At this time, most of my staff was using this Starbucks as an office and meeting place while we remodeled our first campus. We were there all the time, sucking up free wi-fi and getting refills of coffee, so when I met Lindsay the barista, I viewed it as an opportunity to show her the compassion and love of Jesus.

Too many times we expect God to do things for us. We think that because we follow Jesus, he will open up all the doors in our lives so we can easily walk through them. I don't believe that God opens doors the way that we think he does. I believe that God shows us the doors, but it is up to us to open the door and walk through it. Revelation 3:20 says, "Look! I stand at the door and knock. If you hear my voice and open the door, I will come in, and we will share a meal as friends." God shows us where the door is, but it is up to you and me to get up, open the door, and allow him to step in.

In this Starbucks, I felt that God had just shown me a door, so I made sure that I did everything I could to go through it. Trying not to come across as a weird, creepy stalker (not sure if that worked), I paid attention to what hours Lindsay worked, and made a point to always say hi and make small talk with her every time we saw each other. I even took it to the next level and invited her to come check out our church. She told me she was married (she was probably afraid I was interested in her, so I made sure she knew I was married as well) and had a toddler, so I said, "I would love for you and your husband to come, and we have a great kids ministry as well." I was doing anything and everything I could to let this girl know that if she was looking for God to do something in her life, I really wanted her to experience that with us.

She seemed interested and would tell me that she was coming, and then we wouldn't see her that weekend. Then the next time I saw her at Starbucks, we had to fight through the awkward "are you mad at me for not coming?" tone in her voice. I knew this was not about me, so I made a conscious choice to get out of the way so Jesus could get in the way. In those awkward moments, I was always gracious and invited her again to come and check out the church.

After weeks of me harassing her, putting multiple invite cards into her hands, other people inviting her, and even after her own investigation of our website, Lindsay, Chris, and one-year-old Jaxon showed up at our weekend worship experience. All of a sudden, God started working in her heart. I had no idea about the back story of her life, I just knew that God was calling me to reach out to her, but I found out later that Lindsay had lost her brother to a drug overdose during her senior year of high school. After her brother's death, she was mad at God and turned her back on him, despite growing up in a Christian family. During this dark time in her life, running from God, Lindsay got married and divorced, struggled with an eating disorder, began a new relationship with Chris, got pregnant and married again. She was frustrated and upset with God, and was doing everything she could do to fill the God-shaped hole in her heart with everything except God.

I knew none of this when I invited her to be a part of our church. I just saw a girl who was serving me coffee at Starbucks. I had no idea the impact that my compassion would make.

Lindsay's husband, Chris, grew up Jewish, with many different ideas about God and religion, and he was very skeptical of Christianity. If you stumbled into Chris in a back alley, you would probably be a little intimidated. He's got a fierce beard, a hardworking grit about him, and let's just say he knows his way around a tattoo parlor. When he started coming to church with his wife and son, he was obviously uncomfortable about being there, but we kept loving on them, and eventually they kept coming back.

Several months later, Lindsay was experiencing such growth and new-found faith in God that she decided to get baptized. Baptism is a huge celebration for our church – we set up hot tubs in the middle of the mall parking lot and baptize people right out in the open. We do this because we believe baptism is a public declaration of someone's decision to follow Jesus. Lindsay was praying that Chris would get baptized as well, so they could start this new journey with Jesus together as a married couple, but every time she mentioned it to him, he shrugged it off. On the day of baptism, we set up a table with baptism t-shirts, and extra towels and shorts, so that no one has an excuse not to be baptized if God is tugging on their hearts in the moment. Lindsay went up to get her t-shirt, and saw Chris's name on the list to get baptized. She couldn't believe that he had signed up on his own without telling her!

Lindsay and Chris both got baptized in the parking lot of the mall that day – the same mall complex where the Starbucks where she worked is located. They let the old, dead, sin filled people they were go down into the water, and they came up new. Now, Chris is attending Neo Academy, our church's bible college, and training to become a pastor.

I was just like them at one point, saying I would go to church, but being too scared or uncomfortable to actually show up. If I hadn't come past some things in my own life, and realized that it was only by the grace of God, then I might not have had the patience to even care about Lindsay and Chris. I might not have cared enough to pray for her, to find out her work schedule, or to trust God that he loved her more than I did and that I just needed to be faithful. Because of what God had done in my life, I was able to show compassion to Lindsay and Chris, and be a small part of the huge destiny that God has for their lives.

Want to know something else about Lindsay and Chris's story? The first week they ever came to our church, I played a clip from the song "Notorious" by The Notorious B.I.G. (or Duran Duran) in my message. Isn't it ironic? Don't you think? A little too ironic ... yeah, I really do think. (See what I did there? I am a reservoir of musical references. I can't help myself.)

The reason I've told you my story and Lindsay's story is because you won't be able to get through the rest of this book without an understanding of compassion. I was a notorious sinner, and someone cared enough to come after me – one lost kid who no one else thought would amount to anything. When I see others who are lost, I feel compelled to go after them.

This is the gospel at it's core.

Jesus said that he came to seek and save those who are lost.[5] That was good news for me, and it's good news for you as well.

As we move into the rest of this book, we will be unpacking the story Jesus told that unlocks his heart for each of us. As I dive into each chapter and attempt to teach and inspire you as God has taught and inspired me, I want you to have an open heart. If you can remember some of the things that you have come past in your life, then allow God to give you compassion for others. If you are still in a place where you're dealing with your issues, like I was when I first started to discover Jesus, be open to receive compassion and help from someone else, who may have been where you are now. Either way, compassion is essential to the gospel Jesus intended.

CHAPTER TWO

REFLECTION & APPLICATION

How have you been shown compassion?

What have you come past in your life?

List three people to whom you can show compassion starting this week.

Thank God for what he has done in your life, and then ask him to open your eyes to see the people around you who need help or hope.

CHAPTER THREE

PHARISEES, TAX COLLECTORS,
NOTORIOUS SINNERS

TAX COLLECTORS AND OTHER **NOTORIOUS SINNERS** *often came to listen to Jesus teach.* THIS MADE THE PHARISEES AND *teachers of religious law* COMPLAIN THAT HE WAS ASSOCIATING WITH SUCH DESPICABLE PEOPLE — EVEN EATING WITH THEM! SO JESUS USED THIS ILLUSTRATION:

"IF YOU HAD 100 SHEEP AND ONE OF THEM STRAYED AWAY *and was lost in the wilderness,* WOULDN'T YOU **LEAVE THE 99 OTHERS** TO GO AND SEARCH FOR THE LOST ONE UNTIL YOU FOUND IT? *And then you would* JOYFULLY CARRY IT HOME ON YOUR SHOULDERS. WHEN YOU ARRIVED, YOU WOULD *call together your friends and neighbors* TO REJOICE WITH YOU BECAUSE YOUR LOST SHEEP WAS FOUND. *In the same way, heaven will be happier over* **ONE LOST SINNER WHO RETURNS TO GOD THAN** OVER 99 OTHERS *who are righteous* AND HAVEN'T STRAYED AWAY!**"**

Luke 15:1-7

Before we start breaking down Luke 15:1-7, aka "The Parable of the Lost Sheep," we need to understand a little of the context in which Jesus was speaking. Jesus came on the scene at age 30 in the small province of Judea in the Roman Empire. Until then no one really knew who he was, but suddenly he turned some water into wine and he started to become somewhat notorious himself. Some people thought he was the promised Messiah, the savior of the Jews, come to overthrow the Roman Empire and set up his kingdom. Some people thought he was a lunatic (and sometimes I don't blame them because he does and says some crazy stuff ... we'll get into that later); some thought he was a heretic and troublemaker, based on the people he chose to hang out with. And some people weren't really sure yet, but they followed him because his words made them feel alive. Regardless of the differing opinions, no one could disagree that Jesus caused quite a commotion as he traveled around Judea. He did miracles, raised people from the dead, and crowds followed him wherever he went. When he spoke to the crowds, he told stories.

If you can't tell by now, I love telling stories as well. Sometimes they make sense, and sometimes they don't. Just trying to be like Jesus. But seriously, storytelling has been humanity's most enduring form of communication for thousands of years. Even in our modern culture, some of the most powerful messages come through movies and television shows. Facts might tell you what you need to know, but we can only remember so much. Stories stick in your mind and can smack you in the face with truth and understanding years later.

One key element of storytelling is knowing your audience. In Luke 15, there are three different groups of people around to hear what Jesus has to say: Tax Collectors, Notorious Sinners, and Pharisees. After reviewing the New Testament in a broader context than the seven verses that I am focusing on in this book, I discovered that this is the very first time in the story of Jesus' ministry when these three groups are mentioned all in the same place, at the same time, listening to the same message from Jesus. There are other places earlier in the narrative of the Bible where one or two of these groups were present with Jesus at the same time, but never before were they together as one collective audience like they are here in Luke chapter 15.

An important thing to realize about Jesus is that he never did anything by accident. He knew his purpose for being on the earth since the very beginning of time, and while he was here on earth living among us, he was very intentional about everything that he said and did. This makes the audience of these three groups in Luke chapter 15 even more significant. Jesus *intentionally* told this specific story to the Tax Collectors, Notorious Sinners, and Pharisees all at the same time. Even though it was the same parable, it had a very different meaning for each separate group of people. In order to truly understand this significance, and why this story had a different meaning for these three groups, we need to have a better understanding of who exactly these people were in the cultural and spiritual context of their day.

As I break down some of the characteristics of each group, you may recognize similar people in your own life. You may even find yourself looking in the mirror at times, feeling as if you are reading your own profile. As alarming as that might be, don't push those feelings aside, thinking it's the fast food you ate last night. It's the Holy Spirit beginning to tug at your heart, just like he tugged on mine in a very similar way. We will address how to change our hearts, minds, and lives in later chapters, but for now let's just focus on the background in which this life-altering story took place.

NOTORIOUS SINNERS

We've already painted a pretty good picture in chapter one of what it means to be notorious. Notorious sinners were famous for doing terrible things, and committing the worst sins. They were criminals, thieves, liars, murderers, rapists, adulterers: bible-times gangsters. They caused problems everywhere that they went. These people lived their lives doing evil, satisfying their own desires, doing anything they could do that would provide them instant gratification. The quick fix was always best for them.

Notorious sinners refused to deal with truth or consequences; they only pursued what "felt right" and did not worry about anyone or anything but themselves and their own desires. These people loved sinning so much and had done it habitually for so long that it no longer even seemed like it was bad. They actually found more joy in sinning than doing anything else. Sin is like that: You have to keep going deeper and deeper into it to continue getting any pleasure from it.

Not only were notorious sinners self-serving, but they also lacked the ability to take direction from anyone. If they were told to do a task one way, they would blatantly do it the opposite way, simply out of spite. No one ever wanted to be around them, except others like them, who participated in the same destructive behaviors. They were feared, looked down on and shunned. From a spiritual perspective, these people lived their lives in complete darkness. They rejected the law of God and wanted nothing to do with religion. In turn, they were rejected and scorned by the religious.

A final characteristic of notorious sinners was that they were so good at being bad that they negatively influenced those around them to the point that they also became notorious sinners. I used to tell the students in my youth ministry, "Show me your friends, and I'll show you your future." You will always become like those with whom you choose to spend your life.

Once you've established a reputation as a notorious sinner, it's hard to break away from. Pretty soon, that reputation starts to dictate the decisions you make. It defines you, and often you feel comfort from knowing "who you are," what category of society you belong in, and the level of respect or fear that you get for your bad boy rep. If you find yourself falling into this category, take heart – I was there as well. The amazing thing about Jesus, what makes him so controversial, is that many of the notorious sinners who encounter him are changed forever.

TAX COLLECTORS

Tax collectors are mentioned as their own class in society on many occasions in the New Testament. In that day, tax collectors were the most hated people in the world. Think of them as the Internal Revenue Service with even more corruption. The Roman Empire set up people to collect taxes for the emperor in each of its regions, and typically tax collectors were of the same nationality and from the same community as the people they were taxing. We see this in the story of Zaccheus.[1] He was a Jewish tax collector who was appointed by the Roman Empire to enforce the tax code on his Jewish brothers and sisters.

Tax collectors were often described as scum, because it was well known that their policies in collecting the taxes were corrupt and crooked. Because they usually knew the people they were taxing, knew what they did for a living, and knew how much money they had, the tax collectors would over-tax the citizens that they ruled, skimming an extra portion off the top for themselves before sending the tax money to the Roman capital. Sometimes they even went as far as notifying the Roman government who the wealthiest citizens were so that the Romans could enforce an even heavier tax burden on those individuals. I'm sure you can see why no one liked them.

You may have some people that you can identify in your life as tax collectors. They are the people who drain you physically, emotionally, and even spiritually; always taking more than you are willing to offer to them, and taking advantage of you every opportunity that they can find. This could be someone in your family, or even a close friend; someone who has easy access to the "funds" of who you are as a person. You may even be realizing now for the first time that this person has been skimming time or resources off the top of your life for the longest time, leaving you feeling frustrated, exhausted, and confused.

This reminds me of a principle that I learned from my mother, who passionately watches Andy Stanley preach online, and reads many of his books (Andy, if you are reading this and can give us a call, my mother would LOVE to talk to you). She (with insight from Andy Stanley) taught me that, in any relationship, you cannot ask for relational withdrawals unless you are willing to make relational deposits into that relationship. So if someone in your life is always asking for deposits of your time, talents, or finances and never offering anything in return, they are treating you like an open line of endless credit that they never have to pay back. If you don't recognize this unhealthy pattern in your relationship, then that person has the potential to suck you dry.

One example I see in our world of the accumulation of massive amounts of debt with little to no intention to repay is within our Federal Government (let's not make this a political debate, I am simply stating my personal opinion). I don't know about you, but I have no desire for my personal relationships to look anything like this one-sided model of one person doing all of the work, and the other person reaping the benefits. We need to strive for balance in our relationships. If you identify "tax collectors" in your life, I want to encourage you to be honest with yourself and with them. You may need to create boundaries in the relationship, or cut it off for a season. Sometimes tax collectors might not even realize they are living so selfishly. If you can't identify anyone like this in your life, consider yourself blessed, or maybe you need to take a look in that mirror.

PHARISEES

The final group that was addressed in this passage were the Pharisees and teachers of religious law (the Pharisees' scribes). The Pharisees were a sect of Jewish people made up of scholars and religious men who believed they were separate and holier-than-thou because they upheld the entire written and oral law. I'm sure you have heard of the Ten Commandments – Thou shalt have no other gods before me, thou shalt not kill, thou shalt not steal, etc.[2] These were the main part of the commands that God gave to the people of Israel to instruct them on how to live and be blessed. The full law, or Torah (the first five books of the Old Testament), actually contained a total of 613 commands. On top of that, the religious leaders had an oral law that was passed down, containing thousands of additional laws to prevent anyone from breaking one of the other laws. Yikes. I thought Bible college was bad; I would have never made it through Hebrew school.

The Pharisees were very vocal about their beliefs and boasted about their good deeds. They did not hesitate to cast judgment when others were falling short of their impossibly high standards. They were very proud in nature and truly believed that because they held themselves to this high standard of the law, they were actually better than everyone else around them. This attitude of pride was well-known by anyone who came in contact with a Pharisee. Because they were the experts on the law, they didn't actually need God to speak to them about his plans or purpose. They interpreted the commandments to benefit themselves, and set themselves up as examples while condemning others.

When Jesus burst onto the synagogue scene, their world was literally shaken to the core. The Pharisees were so bound by the laws that they couldn't see that they were breaking the first commandment – the law had become their god.[3] Jesus created so much controversy for the Pharisees because he taught the heart of the law, and they only knew the rules of the law. They disagreed with Jesus publicly and privately at every opportunity, but Jesus didn't hold back on what he had to say to them. He called the Pharisees snakes, blind, hypocrites, and white-washed tombs.[4] They looked great on the outside, but inside they were dead and full of impurity, greed, pride, and self-indulgence.

In today's world, we can look at congregations of believers around the world and still find Pharisees sitting right next to us. I have seen people who become members of a church and feel that this entitles them to be involved in every decision the church makes. They put money in the offering plate with a string attached to it, making it known that their generosity gives their opinions more weight than others. They would find themselves overjoyed if their church leadership would take on the mentality of Burger King's tagline, "Have it Your Way."

The modern day Pharisee jumps at every opportunity to be critical, judgmental, or overly opinionated. They think that everyone else around them is living in sin, and that their spiritual gift is to find the fault in a person and then make that person aware of his or her shortcomings. Now I'm sure that none of you reading this book fall into this category, but you can probably think of several people who do (and look, now you are casting judgment, you Pharisee! Gotcha!). Most of us, at one time or another, will experience some Pharisaical tendencies. It may not be to the extreme that I have described, but the truth is: Many of us are much more concerned with our outward appearance than our inner character.

———————

Now that we have an understanding of the three groups in Jesus' audience in Luke chapter 15, let's ponder this passage of scripture. First, under normal circumstances, Tax Collectors, Notorious Sinners, and Pharisees wouldn't be caught dead with each other, so what compelled them to be together in this scene? What was it about Jesus that attracted these polars of society? Second, what did Jesus choose to say when he had an audience with these three groups at once? What did he want them all to know?

Keep these questions in your mind as we dive into the next several chapters. I am going to examine the first seven verses of Luke 15, and share some of what God has taught me through them. Through all the rabbit trails, ADHD streams of thought, and crazy stories, I hope to answer these questions and help you understand, no matter what your past or current situation, how to live out the gospel Jesus intended.

CHAPTER THREE

REFLECTION & APPLICATION

Which group do you identify with? Why?

As either a tax collector, notorious sinner, or pharisee, what is your biggest struggle?

Contact one person you know who may have overcome a similar issue and ask them to help you on your journey.

CHAPTER FOUR

THE GOSPEL OF CHANGE

"TAX COLLECTORS AND OTHER NOTORIOUS SINNERS *often came to listen to Jesus teach.*"

Luke 15:1

Imagine that Jesus was going to come speak at your local church. Throughout the New Testament, we see that Jesus taught in the synagogues on a regular basis, so it's not too far of a stretch to think that he might be scheduled to speak in a church if he was traveling around today. Even if you aren't sure you agree with Jesus' teaching, he's one of the most influential figures in history, so of course you'd want to hear what he has to say. You would get dressed in your Sunday best, and when you entered the church all the regular attendees would be in suit and tie and would nod approvingly to you as you looked for a seat. But then you look over at the person sitting next to you, and it's the homeless drunk you always see walking around downtown, talking to himself. You start to look around at more of the crowd and notice a whole lot of people whom you have never seen in church before. They look like convicted criminals, prostitutes, gang members, drug addicts, and, oh, there's the used car salesman who ripped you off last year ... and before you can stop the thought from forming you think, "Why are they here?"

Whether your attitude was judgmental or simply curious, isn't that what you would ask?

WHY WOULD PEOPLE WHO DON'T LOOK OR ACT LIKE THEY BELONG ANYWHERE NEAR JESUS BE DRAWING CLOSE AND LISTENING TO JESUS TEACH?

But we read in verse one of Luke 15 that this is exactly what was happening. Tax collectors and notorious sinners were coming to listen to Jesus teach, not just once in a while, but all the time.

Maybe they'd heard about Jesus as the bastard from Nazareth, or maybe they'd heard that wherever Jesus went he caused either riots or revival, stirring up trouble of his own kind. Whatever it was, these sinners and fraud artists, who were universally despised, showed up just the way they were – hair a mess, the wrong clothes on, dragging along their vile reputations.

We mentioned earlier that a reputation, even if it's bad, gives you security – people know what to expect from you, and you know what to expect from yourself. But here we see sinners and con artists willing to compromise their notoriety to listen to a young rabbi with what looks like a jaded past. I can almost hear the astonishment in Luke's writing: *Notorious sinners are coming!* The ones we KNOW have no religion apart from themselves, no outward appearance of righteousness, no dealings with God ... but they're coming to Jesus. It would have been much easier for them to continue uninterrupted in their lifestyles of sin, so why did they choose to take a break from the comfort of what they knew to hear a message from this controversial man named Jesus?

Jesus didn't coddle the notorious sinners or tell them they could do whatever they wanted if they just said nice things about him and handed over some money. He offended, challenged, pushed them out of their comfort zone, and made them believe they could change their destiny. They were willing to risk their reputations, which was all they had, in order to hear his message.

Jesus taught a gospel that people had never heard before. He preached, not a gospel of comfort, but a gospel of change. He said to Mary the prostitute, "Go and sin no more."[1] He forgave the sins of a paralyzed man before the man ever asked for forgiveness, and then told him to get up and walk.[2] Never once did Jesus walk someone through a "sinner's prayer." I'm not saying that the sinner's prayer is wrong; I believe that it has a purpose. But when we are more concerned about the repentant words we are saying than the heart transition that is supposed to happen through repentance, we are missing the point.

After Jesus' temptation in the wilderness, he began his ministry by preaching, "Repent, for the kingdom of heaven is near."[3] To repent means to turn from your sins and turn to God; to change the way you think and live. Jesus wasn't concerned with where people had come from or what they had done. He simply called them to change. He offered forgiveness and acceptance and invited people to go on a journey, learning from him as they lived life together.

Jesus never made people jump through hoops in order to receive forgiveness for their sins. Today, sometimes the hardest place to find forgiveness is within the four walls of a church. Some church people like to remember the mistakes, problems, and issues others have, and hold them over their heads. Many churches today have done such a good job of creating a series of hoops to jump through before someone can be considered an acceptable Christian or church member that people who don't "belong" in church are never found anywhere near their buildings.

From the very beginning of his ministry, Jesus modeled the exact opposite of this behavior. He had misfits, sinners, and rejects around him all the time and accepted them exactly how they were. He called his disciples right out of whatever their life-long profession had been. Fisherman and even tax collectors were among the twelve people that Jesus intentionally drew to himself as his closest friends during his three years of ministry on the earth. He told them very simply, "throw down your nets and follow me!"[4] There were absolutely no prerequisites. All that mattered to Jesus was that they were willing to instantly drop everything to follow him. When criticized for the people he was choosing as his closest companions, Jesus said, "Healthy people don't need a doctor – sick people do. I have come to call sinners, not those who think they are already good enough."[5]

Jesus *wanted* the tax collectors and notorious sinners. He knew that his offer of forgiveness, repentance, and change would only appeal to those who were living miserable, empty lives and knew it. The thing about notorious sinners is that, even though they might be very comfortable in their lifestyle, they are usually pretty honest about the fact that they're jacked up. Jesus was offering a chance to start over, a clean slate – something they may have never before thought possible – and his only instruction was "Go and sin no more."

That kind of transformation seems unattainable. I can imagine these notorious sinners and tax collectors hearing Jesus' words and thinking, "He can't be serious. He can't mean me." But as they witnessed this change taking place in people they knew – a tax collector giving money away, a prostitute leaving her adulterous ways, a demon-crazed man becoming sane – they began to believe that maybe this gospel could be for them. So they kept coming back to hear more. They kept coming back and found their hearts were slowly being changed; they found that Jesus' words made them feel alive.

Jesus offers no-strings-attached forgiveness and the promise of a new life to anyone who is willing to lay down their past and follow him. Jesus wants to forgive those who want to be forgiven, who need to be forgiven for the terrible things they've done.

When was the last time you offered a no-strings-attached forgiveness to someone in your life? When was the last time you said to someone, "I know you have issues, I know you have a past, but that's okay. You can still be a part of this journey of discovering the life Jesus can bring."

Jesus loves to call notorious sinners to a life they deemed impossible, and we should be excited about any opportunity we have to help someone experience forgiveness and change.

LISTENING VS. ATTENDING

Something that stands out to me in the first verse of Luke 15 is the word "listen." It says that the tax collectors and notorious sinners were coming to *listen* to Jesus teach. They weren't coming to watch him perform miracles; they weren't there to mock his teaching; they weren't just showing up for no reason. They were there to listen. This made me wonder:

WHAT IS THE DIFFERENCE BETWEEN LISTENING AND ATTENDING?

There are too many people in the United States, and around the world, who are attending church every week just so they can check it off of their to-do list. They attend because they feel obligated, or because it is the "right thing" to do in life, or so their children can grow up in church. The problem is that though they might be warming the church seats with their bottoms, very little of what they hear every week is penetrating their minds. Sadly, even less travels the 18 inches from their heads to their hearts and actually changes who they are as a person.

Many of us wake up on Sunday, roll into church with barely combed hair (at my church we are very grateful if you brush your teeth and put deodorant on, because some people don't) and sit there, trying not to fall asleep, enduring the service with an attitude of indifference. It's like we are playing Russian Roulette with God. We think God has one bullet spinning in the chamber, and if that bullet hits home in our hearts, great! If not, and we get absolutely nothing out of our time at church, we are okay with that as well. If we continue this pattern for a few months, or years, we can begin to think that church is not relevant to our lives at all. As a pastor, this mindset makes me extremely sad, because it is not the heart of God. Jesus and the Holy Spirit are ready and willing to speak to us every single day, if we are willing to listen.

Now, I am not saying that every time you attend a church service that the pastor is going to speak exactly what you need to hear. Maybe you don't have a pastor who is preaching out of the word properly (if this is your situation, I would encourage you to find a place where the truth of the Bible is being taught on a regular basis), but most of the time I think we are too caught up in our own heads to really hear and respond to what God is saying to us. It may not be the preaching that speaks to you, it may be the worship music, or the person who shook your hand when you walked in the door. It may be something as simple as words you read off of the bathroom wall. In my church, the soap dispensers have inspirational quotes on the front of them. I'm not kidding when I tell you that I have had people come up to me and tell me that they were genuinely impacted by a soap dispenser at one of our campuses with the statement "fear paralyzes, but faith has movement." It makes me laugh, but it also has helped me understand that when we open ourselves up to hear from God, he will find creative ways to speak to us and give us hope.

At the Warren City Campus of our church, we have a group of about 20-30 guys who live at the family mission just down the street and attend our worship experience every week. These guys have been drug addicts, drug dealers, pimps, and many of them have been homeless at one point or another. Some of them have experienced a great fall from a successful place earlier in their life to where they are now, sleeping at the mission. We do not judge them, but consider these guys to be as much a part of our church family as anyone else. We are elated that they are hearing the word of Jesus. I love preaching when these guys are in the audience. Not only am I honored to have them attending our church, but when I am preaching, these guys are right there with me the entire time. They're amening and shouting (and, yes, some of their buddies are sleeping right next to them, but that's okay) and they are excited just to be there. They are listening. They are soaking in every word I am saying. They aren't doing this because I am the world's best preacher. They are tuned in because they recognize that I am at a place in my life where they want to be, and the way to get there is by listening, not just attending.

We don't experience change in our lives because we don't listen. Listening in this context doesn't mean simply hearing something with our ears, but taking it into our hearts and applying it to our lives. For us to truly experience the gospel as Jesus intended, we have to be willing to listen and obey when God speaks to us. If we aren't listening when God is talking to us, guess what will happen? He will stop talking. God has provided both the Bible and the Holy Spirit for us to learn to follow his voice. We cannot expect God to drop a brand new word, or a hot-off-the-press revelation into our lives if we aren't even willing to read the Bible, much less do what it says. We need to ask Jesus to open our ears every day; ask the Holy Spirit (who is still God) to activate himself in your life; and finally get into the Word of God (the Bible), the guiding light for your journey through life.[6]

When we are doing these things and really listening for God's voice every day, we will begin to discover that he wants to share secrets with us that no one else has ever imagined. Jesus says over and over again, "anyone who is willing to hear should listen and understand!"[7] Jesus shared his wisdom with the tax collectors and notorious sinners because they didn't just show up, they showed up to listen. If we want the gospel to truly change our lives, we have to stop merely attending church; we have to stop going through the motions of living the Christian life. When we simply attend church on the weekend to check off our to-do list, we receive no lasting effects on our lives. Listening requires that we apply what we are being taught (from the pastor, the soap dispenser, the Bible, or the still small voice of God); and just like the mission guys, and the notorious sinners and tax collectors, listening to Jesus will bring us life.

LOTS OF BRICK & MORTAR, LITTLE LIFE CHANGE

After exploring why notorious sinners were attracted to Jesus, and the difference between listening and attending, I have one final question that begs an answer.

WHY ARE CHURCHES TODAY NOT ATTRACTING NOTORIOUS SINNERS?

Just take a minute and think about a "normal" church. A church is planted in a community, in a building that does not move from place to place every week. The church building is there through rain, snow, or sun (mostly just rain or snow here in northeast Ohio). The church has a budget based on the tithes and offerings of their congregation, which allows church leaders to create support structures for the ministry. They're able to hire specialized staff members for different areas of the church, to outreach the poor, to advance the gospel, and do incredible things for the kingdom.

I thank God regularly for our local church at The Movement. I am so grateful for all the people who give sacrificially to our ministry and enable us to be a vital part of our local community and also communities around the world. Because of the faithfulness and generosity of the people who give to our ministry, we have an amazing staff and we have been able to establish places all over our region where people genuinely encounter Jesus and experience life change in a very real way. We have been incredibly blessed with our local church, and I love it.

But why is it that most local churches have this landmark building that most people in the community recognize, a budget that gives them the ability to do incredible outreaches, and the consistency of a weekly service, yet they still cannot attract notorious sinners the way that Jesus did without any of that?

My answer to this backwards equation is this: What we preach is what we attract. For example, if we are constantly preaching a gospel that centers around barely surviving this life here on earth, we will find that our congregation is a bunch of needy and desperate people, who are looking for religion as a blanket to comfort them until this life is over. If we are preaching a watered down gospel, trying to appease the people with cobwebs on their elbows, who have been attending since the foundation of the church, then we will only attract more people with cobwebs on their elbows who have no motivation to make any lasting impact on our world.

However, if we start preaching like Jesus preached, people will begin to actually experience life change, and the people who need real life change will start to come around. Remember, though, Jesus preached some crazy and controversial messages. Things like "if you want to be my follower, you must hate your father and mother ... and even your own life"[8] or "unless you eat my flesh and drink my blood, you cannot have eternal life."[9] What?!

Jesus preached in a radical way. He was not afraid of offending the religious people, who like a gospel tailored to fit their life. He did not worry about pleasing the crowd with cute anecdotes or inspirational messages. I think he intentionally said some extreme things so that some of the people following him would turn away. After he said the crazy flesh-eating and blood-drinking thing, so many of his followers left that he turned to his twelve chosen disciples and asked, "Are you going to leave me, too?"[10] Jesus wasn't concerned about having the biggest congregation; he wanted the most committed. The gospel Jesus preached was difficult. It was definitely not a gospel of comfort, but of picking up your cross and following Jesus to his death, in order to find life.

This is so far from what most churches today preach. Many times, we focus on preaching what we hate, instead of preaching what we love. When this happens, the church is filled with guilty, fearful people who hate the world, and want to keep all evil, worldly people from corrupting their comfortable Christian community. This is so unhealthy and opposite from the example Jesus set. As the representation of Christ to the world, we should be ashamed that everyone knows what we stand against, but not what we stand for.

Those of us who want to follow Jesus' example of reaching notorious people must be willing to live and preach a gospel that will attract those people. Something about Jesus' gospel, as challenging as it was, attracted the notorious sinners, the rejects and scum of society who had nowhere else to go, and it was with those people that he changed the entire world.

As the vision pastor of The Movement, I choose to be known for what we stand for, not what we are against. I offer forgiveness and acceptance to other people with no strings attached. I believe that is why people who would be afraid to walk into another church choose to walk into The Movement. It's a tough situation to balance, because I don't want to condone sin or encourage people to keep on sinning, but I also don't want to condemn or reject them just because they are at a different point of their journey than I am.

There are a lot of people in your life who do not have the same desire to worship and please God the way that you do. Those people are positioned around you for a reason. God has shown you the doors, and is waiting for you to open them to impact these people, remember? It may not happen the way you think it should, and things may be messier than you expect, but that doesn't give you the right to be critical or condemning. It is our job to love the sinner, and the Holy Spirit's job to convict them of their sin.

I promise you, when we start living and preaching the gospel that Jesus intended, we will start to attract people with notorious backgrounds, who would normally never set foot in a traditional church today.

CHAPTER FOUR

REFLECTION & APPLICATION

Have you been guilty of simply attending church?
If so, why do you think that is?

Have you experienced true life–change because of Jesus?

If not, how can you begin listening and applying God's
words to your life?

Do you think your current lifestyle is one that attracts
notorious sinners? What about your church?

CHAPTER FIVE

HATERS GONNA HATE

"THIS MADE THE PHARISEES AND *teachers of religious law* COMPLAIN"

Luke 15:2a

Have you ever been around someone who is constantly complaining? These people can find something wrong with almost every area of life. They don't make enough money, they deserve a better job, and the grass is always greener on the other side. The list goes on and on ... and on. It's exhausting to be around someone who complains about everything, but if you stay with them long enough you will start to adopt their negative outlook on life.

Maybe you have even come in contact with people like this within the church. Even though all around them lives are being miraculously transformed by Jesus, the complainers are more concerned with the temperature of the auditorium, or the quality of the lighting and video presentation, or that the church didn't serve their favorite cookie after service (and we wonder why notorious sinners think church is a joke). Complainers in the church have a remarkable ability to identify every area of your life that is not up to their standards, and they have no problem calling you out.

This is the exact mindset that we discover with the Pharisees and teachers of religious law in the first part of Luke 15, verse two. In their arrogance, they complained and grumbled about everything that didn't fall into their narrow understanding and interpretation of God's law. Of course, this meant that the Pharisees found fault with almost everything Jesus did, and attacked him on multiple occasions. They complained when Jesus healed a man on the Sabbath, protested when he cast out demons, and criticized the people with whom he associated. Never mind that people were being healed, set free, forgiven, and transformed – all the Pharisees cared about was by whose authority Jesus was performing these miracles.[1]

I have experienced this to some extent in my own journey. I am not claiming to be Jesus (nothing even close to it), but I am doing my best to live the life that Jesus modeled for us. When it comes to the ministry of our church, we are blessed to be able to reach people who are very far from God, but I have often found that some of the people ("church people"), who should be cheering and celebrating and rejoicing with us for the impact we are making for God's kingdom, would rather criticize our methods, nitpick about doctrine, or let me know that they disagree with the way we dress, talk or act. This attitude makes me very sad, because the gospel that Jesus intended is so much more than all of us being carbon copies of each other. I do believe that as Christ followers our spirits should align, we should have similar goals, and a feeling of unity in Christ. I also believe that Jesus and his message are big enough and powerful enough for us to do things differently and still present the truth of the Bible, even if it is in a unique or controversial way. God is a unique God. No two people are created exactly the same; even identical twins have two completely different sets of fingerprints. Psalm 139 tells us that we were "fearfully and wonderfully made."[2] God designed us to be unique, to accomplish his unique purpose. We are not meant to be exactly the same as everyone else.

When Jesus started spending time with notorious sinners and tax collectors, the religious people had plenty to say about it. Jesus was doing something that had never been done before. He was being unique, following the plan that God had laid out for him to accomplish. Jesus was doing things that shook the framework of the traditions and laws that the Pharisees had based their lives upon. Jesus was essentially rocking their world, and they didn't like it because it didn't look like they thought it should.

I recently gave one of my friends an old leadership book to read. Even though the book is twenty-five years old, the principles are still powerful and pertinent today. After a few weeks, I asked my friend what he thought of the book and he said he hadn't read it yet. I was surprised because I had given him two new books previously, and he had devoured them. When I inquired further, he said, "It just looks so dated." I laughed and explained to him that he was missing it. Just because the outside of the book didn't look like what he expected, didn't mean that it couldn't speak into his life.

We all know the old adage: "Don't judge a book by its cover." But we often do.

If we look at our lives today, isn't it true that whenever we do something that others consider to be "not normal," suddenly everyone has an opinion about it? Those opinions quickly morph into complaints, which are usually not even said to your face. These people will complain and gossip about you behind your back, and act like they don't want to hurt your feelings by telling you, but secretly they want you to know exactly how they feel.

One of the best examples of this complaining mindset in our culture today is the news media. The stories that get the most coverage and the most buzz are the ones that are most controversial. These controversial stories are presented, and the invitation is cast to everyone to spout off their opinions and complaints surrounding the issue. Social media has given a voice to everyone, and as I look through my newsfeed more people than not are using their platform to complain.

If we look at the original Greek for the word "complain" in Luke 15:2, it means "greatly murmured." This wasn't just a little gripe session amongst themselves, or a complaint form filed with the synagogue's human resource department. The Pharisees were complaining about Jesus and his ministry in an overly dramatic way that caught everyone's attention. They were posting rants on social media, submitting a thrashing story to the local newspaper, and being interviewed on the national news circuit. If there was one thing these pious law-keepers were good at, it was spreading their complaints and opinions to everyone throughout the land.

Instead of complaining and murmuring, I want to suggest that the response of the Pharisees (and our response when we disagree with something) should have been much different. Even though Jesus was new and controversial, the Pharisees should have taken a step back and waited to see the fruit of Jesus' ministry. Just like you can identify a tree by its fruit, you can tell if a person or ministry is good or bad, healthy or unhealthy, by what they produce.[3] I believe that those of us who consider ourselves to be Christ followers are to live by a higher standard. We should die to our fleshly desires to murmur, complain, and gossip about others. Even on the ministry level, this same principle applies. It is healthy to evaluate each other's fruit or look at how effective another ministry or person is at making disciples and living according to God's word, but when we start criticizing and gossiping about another ministry or another person, we are creating unhealthy patterns that don't line up with the standard and example that Jesus set.

Acts 5:39 speaks about this principle: "But if it is of God, you will not be able to stop them. You may even find yourselves fighting against God."[4] Too many times we point the finger at the way others follow Jesus or do ministry when it differs from what we think is right. The Pharisees, blinded by their devotion to traditions and laws, thought they were doing God's will in setting themselves against Jesus, but the truth is, God does not need us to fight his battles. He is big enough that we are not going to understand everything that he does, so we need to stop complaining and start trusting him. If something is of God, it will last; if it's not, it will pass.

NO HATERS, NO JESUS

Jesus had haters everywhere he went. For those of you who don't know what a hater is, let me give you an urban dictionary version of the definition. A hater is someone who simply can't stand you. They complain about everything you do and can't stand to see you happy or successful, so they are always looking to expose your flaws. Haters aren't necessarily driven by jealousy, they just want to see you fail and take you down a notch. They might not even know why they hate you, they just do. Jesus' main haters were, of course, the Pharisees and other religious leaders of the day. As difficult as it is to have people complaining and spreading rumors about you, if you don't have haters, you're not like Jesus.

Too many times we back off what God has called us to do because we are concerned with what other people are going to think or say about us. But Jesus tells us in John 15, "When the world hates you, remember it hated me before it hated you. The world would love you if you belonged to it, but you don't. I chose you to come out of the world, and so it hates you ... Since they persecuted me, naturally they will persecute you."[5] We have to realize that if we are going to live out the gospel the way Jesus intended and modeled for us, then we are going to experience the same results that he did – not only the amazing miracles, and transformed lives, but also the hostility and persecution.

I know this to be true all to well. I have experienced haters and hatred from many different sources, on many different levels, throughout my years of doing ministry. One of my dear friends who has been a part of my church since it began said to me one time, "Pastor, you've got to know something. When you grow fruit, you attract nuts." I started laughing hysterically, but ever since then it has become one of my catchphrases because it is so true. Many times when a ministry begins to experience success, everyone wants to get a piece of the pie, and often that means people who are a little "off" in their personality or beliefs start coming around. Let me be clear, I am not referring to people with a mental illness; the "nuts" I mean are people who have their own agenda and always want to have the pastor's ear. They try to manipulate the position and platform that God has given you so that it looks like they have accomplished something when in reality they played no part in it at all.

Now don't go out on a witch hunt for someone in your life who might be trying to control you or steal your influence. I just want to raise your awareness to the fact that when you decide to follow Christ and his calling there will be people who come out of the woodwork who want to offer "guidance" that might be more self-serving than godly.

When we first started our church, we were meeting in the conference room of an office building. During those early days, we had a guy show up who seemed a little odd. We treated him with love, accepted him into our group, helped him buy groceries, and even paid for him to attend events with us. But as time went on I began to notice that he was acting in ways that I, as vision pastor and leader of the church, felt were inappropriate. This man was older and single, and he would often pull young girls into conversations, even going as far as prophesying and laying hands on them in isolated situations. He often pulled leaders out of group conversations to have one-on-one talks about his struggles or how God had given him a word to share that could only be shared from the platform. He hinted many times that he needed to preach and share with the whole church, and I explained that we only allowed our pastors to speak on the weekends, which led him to begin giving me instruction on what I should be teaching and praying for in our services. Through all of this and more, we were very gracious to this man, even though we became increasingly uncomfortable with the way he acted.

On one particular Saturday night, he was talking very loudly in the back of our small conference room during the middle of our service. It was very distracting to the other 70-80 people in the room, so I approached him, placed my hand on his elbow and respectfully asked him to step out into the hall as the service wrapped up. Soon after that, I received an email from him that accused me of manhandling and forcing him out of our facility, which was, in my personal opinion, a bit of an exaggeration. I replied that I was sorry he felt the way he did and requested a face to face meeting. Instead, he continued to communicate through email, and to this day, I regret that I let that email conversation continue.

In my immaturity as the pastor of a brand new church, I was trying to help this man whose only goal (as I later discovered) was to run me out of my position. He said very hateful things to me and made outrageous accusations. For example, he claimed that our church could only be growing because we were making deals with the devil for our finances, that we were corrupt and God would never bless us, and even that I had been divorced (which was news to me). He demanded references for my ministry qualifications, stating he had proof that I had been fired from every church I had ever pastored (which is false; although I was kicked out of bible college at age 20, I have never been fired from any pastoral position I have held).

I'm not saying these things to defend myself, I just want to clarify how deeply this hurt me. In those early days when our church was just starting to grow, I felt like I could be personally invested in the life of every person who walked through our doors, and I was. This situation cut me so deeply because I felt very betrayed. I had done my best to show love to and share wisdom with a difficult person, who was now countering with hate and lies. It was the first time in my life I was being accused of things that had no foundation in truth.

Now if you recall the bus story from chapter one, you know I have been accused of things in my past. Back then I had a reputation, and whenever there was trouble it wasn't a far stretch to assume that I had been there. But years later, after I had worked hard to build my character and become a person of integrity, it was hard to swallow allegations that I knew were 100% fabricated. Imagine how Jesus felt as he stood silently before the Jewish high council as false testimony after false testimony was hurled against him.[6]

By the grace of God, and with the help of two of our other pastors, I was able to deal with this man and find resolution for the situation. This was the first time, of many times now, that I have publicly or privately encountered complaints and gossip about me, and I do not expect it to be the last. When you decide to go all in for Jesus, the devil notices, and he's not happy about it. The enemy will do everything in his power to whisper to the hearts of people, both sinners and saints, to disqualify you from the call that God has on your life. I have learned that the more I say yes to God and continue to follow his plan, the louder the haters and critics become.

OVERCOMING HATERS

When we decide to follow Jesus despite the complaints and murmurings of religious (or even unbelieving) people around us, the question is not if but when, you will start getting haters. At some point in our lives and journeys with Jesus, we are guaranteed to cross paths with someone like this. People will hate us just because we love Jesus. In order to deal with this adversity, we need to have a resolve and a thickness to our skin that allows us to respond in love and in confidence that we are living the way God has called us to live.

In order to develop that resolve we must first go to Jesus and draw strength from him, before we go to anyone else. Before reacting to a person or a situation, take time alone to pray and ask God to allow you to see that person the way that he sees them. God is love, and therefore he can look at every one of us and love us unconditionally, no matter what we may have said or done. We need to learn from God how to have this same outlook, even with those who blatantly hate us.

The second thing to do when you are dealing with haters is to find tangible ways to bless your enemies. Jesus said, "If someone slaps you on one cheek, turn the other cheek. If someone demands your coat, offer your shirt also ... Do you think you deserve credit merely for loving those who love you? Even the sinners do that!"[7] There will be times in our lives that our enemies will be in need. We may notice it on social media or hear about it from another person, but if we are open to it, God has a funny way of bringing to our attention that we need to serve and care for those who hate us. I have won over some of my very worst enemies just by loving and serving them. This process is extremely difficult because the entire time my flesh (my human desires and thoughts) is screaming at me, reminding me how they have used and abused me. When we choose to serve our enemies, and not gossip about them, and not match their hate with more hate, we become more like Jesus.

In Psalm 23, King David talks about God preparing a feast for us in front of our enemies.[8] This is not a meal where we sit above our enemies in a boastful way and make them look like idiots. Rather, it is God showcasing in front of everyone who is coming against you that He provides, protects, and stands for someone who will serve, love, and honor their enemies. If God can find that quality in you, then he will provide everything you need at the table in front of all those who are criticizing you. And as God is elevating us to that place of honor and respect, the end goal is that our enemies will see the blessing of God upon our lives, and they will in turn want to change the way they live and become like Jesus themselves.

If we will respond in this way, we will keep our hearts in line with Jesus. Jesus went as far as dying on a cross for those Pharisees and religious teachers who mocked him, taunted him, and accused him throughout his entire ministry. As he was hanging on that tree, Jesus cried out with his last breath, "Father, forgive them, for they don't know what they are doing."[9] Jesus is the ultimate example for us to follow. Even though "haters gonna hate," we must still respond in love.

My final encouragement to you is to not be afraid of the hate, the accusations, and the complaints when they come, but rather to welcome the opportunity to evaluate your heart, love your haters, and grow from the experience.

Stand confidently when there are people trying to tear you down and destroy what God is building in you. You can thank God because you are getting your affirmation that God is working on your behalf. As long as everything you are doing can be backed up in the Word of God, no opinion or hatred will stand against you. If what people are saying to you or about you does not have Biblical backing, you don't have to listen to it. Stand firm and know that when trials and tribulations come, God is using them to work something out in you, preparing you for the next stage of the journey he has for your life. Don't freak out when adversity comes, embrace it. Don't worry when people talk bad about you, because they did the exact same thing to Jesus. Stand up and be who God has made you to be and know this: You are only responsible for what God tells you to do; you are not responsible for how others respond. Haters gonna hate, but you can choose to rise above and follow God's destiny for your life, no matter what it costs.

CHAPTER FIVE

REFLECTION & APPLICATION

List 3 haters in your life.

Why are they hating you? Is there some truth to their accusations?

How can you serve them?

Is there someone that you hate, or that you secretly want to fail? Remember, the world hears your words, but God sees your heart.

CHAPTER SIX

GET UNCOMFORTABLE

"THAT HE WAS ASSOCIATING WITH *such despicable people* – EVEN EATING WITH THEM!"

Luke 15:2b

In the last chapter we discussed the first part of Luke 15:2 where the Pharisees are complaining and hating on Jesus. What was Jesus doing that made them so upset? We find the answer in the second part of the verse. Two words: *associating* and *eating* with despicable people (the notorious sinners and tax collectors). This may not seem like a big deal to us now, but it has huge implications.

ASSOCIATING VS. TOLERATING

Several times in my life, I have found myself in situations that caused others to complain about the people with whom I was associating. Recently, a friend of mine who is a musician was playing in a local bar. This was not a bar like

Applebee's Neighborhood Bar and Grill. This bar was more like Hood Rat's Don't-Tell-Your-Momma-You-Are-There-Hole-In-The-Wall Bar. But my friend was playing there, and he had actually invited me, even though I really don't think he expected me to show up. I knew that he was going through a rough patch in his life, having fallen from a strong relationship with Jesus to a place of questions and doubts, so I decided to be intentional about supporting him and showing him that I really cared about him.

When he saw my wife and me walk in, I could tell that he was shocked to see us in that place. My wife and I quickly discovered that all the regular tables and chairs were occupied, leaving us with only one option for seating – the bar. Sitting on our bar stools, we were surrounded by the classic bar scene from every movie – guys who worked hard all week at a blue collar factory, blowing their paychecks, knocking back beer after beer. And here I was, just finished preaching to our church at our Saturday night worship experience, and now the good ol' boy next to me was trying to buy me a round.

It was hard not to feel uncomfortable in that environment. I remember the battle raging in my mind. I was a young pastor with a brand new church, whose reputation in the community was still being formed, and I couldn't stop myself from wondering, *Is this appropriate? What if someone recognizes me? Am I going to get in trouble for this? How will this affect my reputation?* I had to fight these thoughts because I knew my intention for being there was not to get drunk to forget all my problems. My goal was to encourage this guy, who was struggling with faith and had felt judged by many other Christians for performing in bars.

Of course, just as I was feeling good about being at this bar, immediately someone came up behind me and said, "Pastor, this is the last place I would expect to see you!" Great, I'd been caught. I had never met the person, but they had seen me in a ministry environment at some point. I smiled and made a joke. After a short conversation, the person returned to his table and I was plunged back into my mental battle. In that moment I decided that, even though I had no idea what would be said about me later and rumors might fly all over the place and #PastorDougSpottedAtBar might start trending on social media, I was not going to live in constant fear of what others were thinking or saying about me.

I can tell you this, if you choose to allow the thoughts and opinions of others to dictate your life, you will be miserable. You will be unhappy all the time and constantly worrying, which directly contradicts the challenge of Philippians 4:6 to "not worry about anything, instead pray about everything." Before I even walked into that bar, I prayed and asked God to examine my heart. I felt no check in my heart from God – my motivation was pure, and I was doing nothing wrong. When my friend had finished playing, we ended up having a great conversation, and were the last people to leave the bar that night. If I had given in to the fear of others' opinions of me, I would not have had that opportunity to connect with my friend.

I think one of the most difficult struggles that a follower of Christ faces today is the modern Christian ideas that we should be "in the world, not of the world" and "avoid the appearance of evil." Both of these phrases are formed from scriptures (John 17:14-18; 1 Thessalonians 5:22), but when we actually examine the passages and the life of Jesus,

NOTORIOUS

I think we have taken them out of context and applied them to the Christian life in a way that has made us afraid to associate with "the world." In John 17, Jesus is actually saying the opposite of what this phrase implies. He says that we do not belong to the world, just as he does not, but he is sending us into the world, for the same purpose that he was sent. He wants us here!

I believe there is a balance we have to learn when we begin to step out into uncomfortable situations and reach the people that no one else is reaching. I have seen many pastors and ministries compromise their integrity and calling just to be more relevant to the world, but I have also seen many professing Christians miss opportunities to be a light in a dark place because they were afraid of appearing evil. We can maintain this balance by staying close to the heart of God, and keeping his commandments – loving him first above everything and everyone, and then loving others. Jesus spent a lot of time alone with his Father, developing a strong relationship and the ability to know the Father's voice, so that even when he was tempted, he never sinned.[1]

Years ago I stumbled upon this quote that has stuck with me, and captures this idea so well:

> "I'm always amazed at an aspect of Jesus' ministry that's so obvious, but which we often miss. He partied with sinners and never sinned; he touched the unclean without becoming dirty; he healed the sick, but didn't catch any of the diseases. I take his example as a mandate to mingle with the culture I'm a part of without undue fear of being contaminated."[2]

Jesus didn't seem to care that he was being associated with sinners. He didn't sweat the fact that a lot of people were probably thinking that he was just as bad as the people he hung out with. He was called a drunkard, a glutton, the friend of sinners, and more.[3] But he knew he wasn't any of those things, nor was he afraid of slipping into sin and becoming like the people that he welcomed into his life. He knew who he was and he knew who God said he was, so he didn't care what anyone else thought.

The religious leaders constantly called Jesus' actions and associations into question because he was always doing things they didn't understand. He was frequently in places that made them uncomfortable, because a good Jewish rabbi shouldn't be in those places or with those people. Sometimes I wonder if the Pharisees were so critical of Jesus because they knew what an asset he could have been to their religious agenda. At age 12, Jesus was found in the Temple discussing deep questions with the religious teachers for three days, and his understanding and answers were blowing their minds.[4] Crowds were amazed with how he taught the scriptures with so much authority. Don't you think that it's possible that when they first encountered Jesus, the Pharisees were interested in getting him to be on their side? I imagine them feeling like the Cleveland Cavaliers when they had the number one draft pick in 2003, and LeBron James, who grew up only 40 miles away, was in the draft. The Pharisees probably couldn't understand why someone who, in their eyes, had so much potential would choose to waste his time with the scum of the earth.

But this was exactly what Jesus was doing. He intentionally chose to be associated with despicable people.

An association with another person means that you are connected to them in a way that other people notice. To associate yourself with someone means that the outside observer will assume that you have the same values and convictions as that person. Other translations say Jesus was receiving or welcoming sinners, but either way, he created a connection that basically said, "We're on the same team." When I was present at that bar, even though I was not indulging in the activities and actions that environment offered, I was still associated with everything it represents.

Our culture creates hysteria over who is associating with whom. From the media and tabloids plastered with celebrity gossip of who was seen where to school and workplace social caste systems, we place so much value on our public perception, careful to associate ourselves with the right people and places so others won't get an idea about us that isn't quite accurate. We even wear certain brands of clothing or drive a certain kind of car because we want to be associated with what that brand or car represents. Jesus seems to have put very little value on his public image. Oh, he was very intentional about who he associated with, but he wasn't worried what the rest of the world thought about it.

When we make the choice to be associated with notorious sinners, it is going to be controversial, and it is going to be difficult. We have to guard ourselves from begrudgingly walking through this process. There is a difference between associating with someone like Jesus did and just tolerating a notorious sinner because it is the right thing to do.

We live in a culture that supports tolerance. We are continually being asked to tolerate other people's beliefs and lifestyles and actions when they differ from our own. We don't have to agree, we just have to tolerate. A working definition for the word "tolerate" is to painfully endure, put up with, or allow the existence, occurrence, or practice of something you don't like, without interference. This is very different from associating with someone. In association, we are accepting someone into our lives, and they are reciprocating in the same way. Association is a two-way street; a relationship of tolerance is a dead end.

If we get honest with ourselves for a minute, we will probably realize that alarmingly we tolerate people around us all the time without even realizing it. We will talk to people or sinners if we have to, but we aren't interested in having a genuine connection with them. We aren't interested in knowing the story of how they ended up where they are, and we certainly aren't willing to open up the book of our life and start sharing stories of our own experiences with them. Jesus was not *tolerating* these despicable people. Jesus was *associating* with some of the worst people that he could find.

Tolerance says, "What you're doing is okay for you, but I don't want to be a part of it."

Association says, "I accept you; I'm one of you; I understand you; and because of that, I can show you how to be better."

Jesus was so connected to the Father and so confident in his mission that he wasn't afraid of the "bad influence" of notorious sinners. Instead, he effected change in people. He didn't condone their sin, but by associating himself with them, he took their sin on himself and gave them the chance to see a different way to live.

Who are you willing to be associated with in order to be like Jesus? What are you willing to be labeled or branded as in order to accomplish the mission Jesus has given you? Are you willing to give up your reputation or social status to reach the people that no one but Jesus wants?

My heart's desire (because of what Jesus has done for me and in me) is to reach the unreachable, and sometimes that might take me to places that make other people uncomfortable. However, I know that by associating myself with notorious sinners, rather than just tolerating them, I can knock down the walls of separation that have been built so high between sinners and saints.

When we were getting ready to plant our church, my wife and I started to work secular jobs, so that we didn't have to take salaries from the church, and all of the funds the church received could go right back into the ministry. It was difficult to be bi-vocational, but that's what we felt was right. So for a year and a half, I was pastoring a new church and working in the human resources department of a national pallet company to pay the bills. In my HR position, I oversaw the staffing for four different facilities and was responsible for about 150 employees. I was actively involved in the hiring, training, and termination processes for these employees, as well as troubleshooting daily issues that arise with multiple people working together under the same roofs.

The word spread among the employees that I was a pastor who was starting a new church, and I was labeled as the "pastor guy." For many of them, this created a lot of preconceived ideas about the kind of person I was, and I felt that part of my job (outside of my regular HR duties) was to help reshape their idea of what a Christ follower looked like.

I wanted them to see that not all Christians are uptight and judgmental. I desired to show these guys that people who love Jesus could be easygoing, relatable, and capable of loving people who don't agree with us.

At one of my facilities, there was one young man who was outspoken about not liking Christians. He told people to pass information on to me that he was a devil-worshipper and was involved in occult practices. He wanted both to rile me up and give me reason to avoid him completely, so that I wouldn't try to force my faith down his throat. After catching wind of this situation, the first thing I did was begin to pray for him. My prayer was very simple and honest. "God, this young man is hurt; how can I help? What are you asking of me in this situation?" From then on, I began to intentionally associate myself with this guy (and not just tolerate him from afar). The first few times that I walked up to him and shook his hand or tried to communicate with him, it did not go well. I would greet him and ask how his day was going, and he would mumble unintelligible words in response. I did not let that affect me, though. This wasn't about me; it was about opening a door for Jesus to get ahold of this guy's heart.

We continued these awkward interactions for quite a while, until one day when his car broke down and he was unable to get to work on time. After borrowing a car and making it to work, the rumor spread fast that he didn't have enough money to pay for the repairs needed on his vehicle. Now, the company I worked for actually had money earmarked to help employees in times of need, and my position allowed me some discretion to distribute these funds if I encountered an employee who needed help. With some moving and shaking on my end, I was able to fast-track the process of accessing the money for this guy's car repairs. I didn't have to do this, but I chose to help him because I knew that a tangible demonstration of compassion would be more powerful than anything I could ever say to him.

When I approached him and gave him the money to fix his car, I simply shared that God loved him, and that I cared about him and wanted to make sure his needs were met. He was dumbfounded that I was helping him when he had made such an effort to avoid me. In the days and weeks that followed that interaction, things were different than they had been before. When I saw him at the lunch table, he would sit a little closer to me and start a conversation instead of sitting in a completely different area. When I was on the floor making my rounds, he would make a point to wave and say hello.

This change would not have happened if I had decided simply to tolerate this guy or not to show him compassion. Since I had chosen to associate with him and offer him as much compassion as I could, God was able to do what he does best. God used me to show a self-proclaimed devil-worshipper what a true follower of Christ looked like. Even though I don't know where this young man's heart is today, I do know that I was faithful in exposing him to the real Jesus, who loves and embraces notorious sinners.

LET'S EAT

It's easy to understand why the Pharisees didn't like the fact that Jesus was welcoming and accepting tax collectors and notorious sinners, but why did they make such a big deal about eating with them?

We are so overexposed to food access today that it's hard to even understand the culture of food that existed during the Bible times. There were no restaurants. No McDonald's, no Subway, no Chipotle – nothing. There was only a market where you could go to buy the things that you did not grow or raise for yourself at home. Once you got your items home, there was no refrigeration system. The things you bought would have to be eaten within a few days of purchasing them, or they would go bad. Gathering and preparing food was a daily chore, and in most cases food was eaten for survival and not mere enjoyment. The opportunity for obesity was rare in this culture because resources were so scarce, and most people were poor. If you were overweight back in those days, people knew you were rich and powerful.

With this framework in mind, we can begin to view Jesus eating with these despicable people in a different light. We know that Jesus did not pull a couple of them aside and offer to take them out to the local burrito shop and pay for their lunch. That was not an option. In order for Jesus to eat with someone, he had to show up to their house. He would be welcomed into someone's private home and assisted in washing his feet (the roads were made of dirt and people wore only sandals, so their feet got very dirty), and then they would share a meal together.

As a pastor, I have been invited to eat at many people's houses. I usually try to set up dinner meetings at public restaurants, rather than personal homes, because I never know what to expect. I could end up on a scene of the next "Hoarders" episode. This has never happened (yet), and most of the time people are very hospitable. However, it can be uncomfortable to enter into a stranger's house and spend time with their family and eat the food they cook and wonder how long you should stay so as not to appear rude but also not overstay your welcome.

In those days, people did not invite just anyone into their homes. You were only invited in if you were family or a close friend. In a society with much different class separations than we have now, where eating was considered one of the most intimate things you could do with other people, you weren't supposed to eat with people who were a different ethnicity or religion or social status. When you ate with someone, it meant there was a bond of trust and mutual approval in the relationship. The fact that Jesus was invited into the houses of notorious sinners and tax collectors really shows us an insight into how they viewed Jesus. They trusted Jesus and accepted him as one of their own because he was intentional about reaching them despite their reputations.

Consider also how these tax collectors and notorious sinners would have paid for the food. We established earlier in the book that most of a tax collector's money came from scamming his countrymen, so there is a good chance that they were feeding Jesus with food paid for by money they had stolen from someone else. I bet the Pharisees had a field day with that one! No wonder they were disgusted that Jesus, a young teacher who they probably wanted on their side, was sharing meals with blatant sinners and entering into the homes of the worst of the worst.

Yet, in the story of Zacchaeus, when Jesus invited himself to be a guest in Zacchaeus' home, it totally changed Zacchaeus' heart. You can check out the story in Luke 19. After sharing a meal with Jesus in his home that day, Zacchaeus, a wealthy tax collector, decided to give half his money to the poor, and pay back everyone he had cheated four times over. Jesus' response is so powerful, "Salvation has come to this home today ... For the Son of Man (i.e., Jesus) came to seek and save those who are lost."[5] Crazy how someone's life could be changed just by eating with Jesus!

Imagine what it would be like if your hospitality changed someone's perspective on God. Imagine what could happen if you were intentional about associating with the person who no one else thought was worth it. Yes, you might experience rejection, it might cause others to question your sanity or morals, or it might cost you your reputation. But you need to ask yourself how the principles that Jesus modeled so perfectly can begin to be a part of who you are as a person, and imagine what it would be like to live out the gospel as Jesus intended – not for your own gain or comfort, but for someone else's.

CHAPTER SIX

REFLECTION & APPLICATION

Who is God asking you to associate or share a meal with?

Who do you need to be intentional about spending time with, even if it causes your reputation to be questioned?

Was there someone who reached out to you and showed you Jesus' love when you didn't feel "worthy" of it?

Maybe instead of giving a homeless person $5, buy a sandwich for them and spend a few minutes listening to them and making them feel valued.

CHAPTER SEVEN

A SIMPLE STORY

"*So Jesus used this*
ILLUSTRATION:"

Luke 15:3

In a landmark 1944 study, 34 humans were shown a short film and asked what was happening in it. The film showed two triangles and a circle moving across a two-dimensional surface. The only other object onscreen was a stationary rectangle, partially open on one side.

Only one of the test subjects saw this scene for what it was: geometric shapes moving across a plane. Everyone came up with elaborate narratives to explain what the movements were about. Typically, the participants viewed the triangles as two men fighting and the circle as a woman trying to escape the bigger, bullying triangle. Instead of registering inanimate shapes, they imagined humans with vivid inner lives. The circle was "worried." The circle and the little triangle were "innocent young things." The big triangle was "blinded by rage and frustration."[1]

In this study, people saw simple shapes on a short film and transformed them in their minds into something very real. Why did they do that? Because we are wired to interact with and think about our world through stories. We live for stories. The shapes these people were seeing had no narrative, no plot lines, no nothing, but all except one provided wild explanations about what was happening on the screen. Our brains are hard-wired for creativity, and we are taught from a young age to think about our world through the lens of a Disney princess or a Jedi knight. Whether from books, movies or television shows, stories shape who we are.

If you look at the history of the New York Times best seller list, you will discover that the manual for your vacuum cleaner has never made that list. Most of you probably don't read manuals of any type, unless absolutely necessary, because it is just dry, boring information with no bad guys, no good guys, and nothing to capture your attention (I even struggle with making sense of IKEA furniture manuals, and they're just pictures). Instead, we read the same storybooks over and over again to our children and get lost in fictional narratives, even when we already know the endings. Even those who prefer non-fiction (like me) are often reading the stories of other people's lives, or reading about how to improve the story of their own life. If you are one of those people who hates reading (first of all, congratulations for making it to chapter seven of this book), you're probably addicted to a certain television series, film genre, or even a video game that allows you to digitally live out an epic adventure. Stories help us remember a time in our life when we didn't have a care in the world, and they also help us forget the many cares we deal with every day.

Stories can also remind us of something we lost and need to recover. Think about this: Little boys dream of being strong heroes and defeating a great enemy; little girls long to be beautiful heroines worth fighting for, caught up in a great adventure. Of course, we all grow up and are taught the difference between fantasy and the cold, harsh reality of life. But I think deep down, we all feel a little disappointed because we know we were meant for something more. Truth trumps "reality" as we understand it, and the truth is that we are part of an epic story that God has been writing since before time began. Good versus evil, the fall of humanity, a Savior, a great battle, and the promise of happily ever after. We see this pattern in almost every story we know. As people created in the image of God, it's built into our DNA to tell stories and to live out stories that reflect the ultimate story of redemption.

So when Jesus, the long awaited Messiah, stepped into the story, what did he do? He started telling stories. For hundreds of years, the Jewish people were forming their own opinions of God and how he operated (people are still doing this today), passing down the old stories of Adam and Eve, Noah and the ark, Moses delivering the Israelites from slavery in Egypt and leading them to the promised land, but until Jesus showed up, they hadn't heard from God or seen him work on their behalf for something like 400 years. Jesus wanted them to know what God the Father is really like, what the kingdom of heaven means, and what it means for them to experience salvation and redemption – because it is all going to look very different from what they've been expecting. He knew they wouldn't understand, so Jesus used simple stories to illustrate moral and spiritual principles.

Jesus knew that humans learn best through stories (after all, he was there when we were created), and will relate to them even if we don't immediately grasp their significance. As I said in chapter three, stories stick in your mind and can smack you in the face with truth and understanding later. Before we dive into the meaning of the specific illustration Jesus used in the passage found in Luke 15, I want to set up the significance of the way Jesus chose to teach.

A parable is a story about earthly, everyday situations that has a heavenly meaning. Through parables, Jesus taught about love, forgiveness, heaven, character, expectations, and judgment. We can count over 58 parables throughout the first three gospels of the New Testament (Matthew, Mark, and Luke). If we can understand them and apply them to our lives, parables shape how we should live as part of God's kingdom on earth. Parables are a big deal, and it's important to note that Jesus chose to teach the lesson of Luke 15 through not one, but three similar illustrations.

If Jesus would have taught in the style of your vacuum manual, most people would not have connected with him on the levels that they did. Even though Jesus had haters, there were always crowds following him, waiting to hear what he was going to say next. He spoke with authority, and the people were entertained and intrigued. I'm willing to bet that the mystery of not quite grasping exactly why he was telling some of these stories made them even more memorable.

As human beings, we will never fully understand all the things of God until we are one day united with him in heaven, and Jesus knew that. If we break down Jesus' intentions for teaching through parables, we can find two specific goals. First, Jesus used parables to *conceal* truth from the multitudes, who were merely interested in his celebrity. Second, he used parables to *reveal* truth to those who wanted his substance, by comparing truth to something they could understand.

In Matthew 13, Jesus tells his disciples that he speaks in parables to the crowd because even though the crowds see what Jesus does, and hear what he says, they don't really understand, nor do they want to.[2] Many times, we are so entrenched in our own ideas about God and reality that we reject the truth when we hear it. Maybe we've been taught that God is like a genie in a bottle, but he hasn't provided for us like we thought he should, so we resent him. Maybe we've been deceived into thinking that God is angry and destructive, out to ruin our lives, so when bad things happen we blame him. Maybe we believe that God is a nice old grandfather with a white beard (kind of like Santa Claus) who will give us presents once a year, but mostly stays out of the way and lets us do what we want, so we ignore him. Most of us grow up with preconceived ideas about God and what he expects based on our experience with our fathers and the opinions of others that are probably far from the truth. For that reason, our hearts can be so hardened towards God that we will often reject anything that sounds like it could be God trying to reach or change us. It was the same then; Jesus concealed the truth about the kingdom and the Father in stories, so that the crowds wouldn't automatically tune out and be judged for rejecting it.

However, this also allowed Jesus to separate the crowds that were following him because it was the new, exciting thing to do from those who were really seeking to understand and follow his teaching. He often revealed the deeper spiritual truths to his disciples when they asked him later what the parables meant. Of course, sometimes they still didn't get it, but Jesus knew that someday they would. Later, they would have the Spirit of God with them and in them who would remind them of the things that Jesus taught and reveal to them how to apply those stories and truths to their lives.[3]

Ultimately, I know this about stories: They work. Whether they connect us to a memory or teach us what to expect in life or stir up an emotional response, stories can get us through some of the hardest parts of life.

When the movie *Marley and Me* came out in theaters, I went with one of my friends to see it. It was a little weird for two guys to walk into a movie theater filled with children and their parents – my 6-foot-3, 230 pound buddy certainly looked out of place – but we loved dogs, and this was a movie about a dog. When the movie began, it was just what we expected. We were laughing and enjoying the story about a guy, played by Owen Wilson, who didn't want a dog, but got one for his family and how Marley (the dog) through his hilarious antics and unwavering loyalty, weaves his way into the guy's heart as they experience all the changes that life brings. Good, right? My friend and I were loving it. Until we got to the end (SPOILER ALERT: If you have never watched *Marley and Me*, I'm about to tell you what happens at the end of the movie).

You expect a family-friendly movie like this to leave you feeling good at the end, but just when all the characters have reached a place of stability and happiness, Marley gets sick. By this time, he is very old and won't come inside (when dogs are about to die, they often want to stay outside to put some separation between themselves and their "pack"). So, in a last ditch effort to save his best friend, Owen Wilson drives Marley to the veterinarian, telling him on the way that he didn't want Marley to die. But there was nothing the vet could do. It was Marley's time to go. Remembering their journey together from the time Marley was a puppy, Owen Wilson's character breaks down crying, as the vet puts Marley to sleep. The entire family in the movie is crying over the loss of their pet, and so was pretty much everyone in the theater.

I remember tears streaming down my face and thinking that in the pitch black theater, my masculinity would remain intact as long as I didn't make the sniffle noise. When you're crying that much your nasal passages get clogged and runny, and there is no way to breathe without loudly inhaling your own snot (I'm just being real; you know it's true). In the darkness of a movie theater, the number one indicator of crying is the sniffle, because it's too dark to see anyone's face. As I was doing my very best to not make the sniffle noise, I began to hear the exact sniffle I have described rising from the seat next to me. My 6-foot-3, motorcycle-riding, never-expresses-emotion buddy was weeping without shame, at the death of a fictional dog. We might have been crying more than some of the children and mothers in the theater with us.

I remember being surprised at how emotional I was, because in my mind I knew that all dogs die (and go to heaven – heyo! more early 90s references), and I had even experienced the loss of my own dog in the past. Yet sitting in the theater that day, I was moved beyond my rational thought by a compelling story.

To this day, I have never watched *Marley and Me* again, but I remember the story vividly, and I remember how it made me feel. Stories have this ability to soften even the hardest hearts. Stories can even open up the opportunity for healing to take place inside of us, or inspire us to change. We remember them years later, and pass them along to other people. Jesus' parables were a vehicle for him to reach the unreachable and teach the unteachable. As we read the story Jesus chose to share with the notorious sinners, tax collectors, and Pharisees, my prayer is that you will be able to understand what Jesus is saying specifically to you through this illustration.

CHAPTER SEVEN

REFLECTION & APPLICATION

What are some stories that have brought about change in your life?

How did they make you feel?

How have you passed those stories on to others?

CHAPTER EIGHT

LET'S TALK ABOUT SHEEP

> **"IF YOU HAD 100 SHEEP AND ONE OF THEM STRAYED AWAY** *and was lost in the wilderness,* **WOULDN'T YOU LEAVE THE 99 OTHERS TO GO AND SEARCH FOR THE LOST ONE UNTIL YOU FOUND IT?"**
>
> *Luke 15:4*

In just the first sentence of this parable, there are five different principles that I believe we need to understand. These are the thoughts that God revealed to me as I explored this passage; these are the concepts that begin to reveal the gospel that Jesus truly intended.

BAAA, BAAA, BLACK SHEEP

I find it very interesting that Jesus chose to use sheep for this illustration. He could have used goats or camels or any other animal that was living in the land of Judea during his day. But Jesus chose sheep. Everyone who would have heard this parable was familiar with sheep, whether they had raised them, or used their wool to make fabrics and clothing, or ate their meat, or used them in bartering transactions. Sheep were an essential part of life in Biblical culture, but nowadays we rarely encounter sheep unless we grew up on a farm or visit the annual county fair. So, we need to understand a few things about these creatures in order to grasp Jesus' analogy.

Sheep are fearful animals, and they are very easily spooked. It may seem irrational, but sheep consider almost any living or moving thing that passes in front of them as a predator. It could be a leaf. Doesn't matter. Sheep will freak.

Because of this, sheep have a herd mentality. Being in a group creates the feeling of security as they roam the hills. Sheep become very stressed when isolated; they actually need to be around other sheep in order to feel comfortable.

Despite this group mentality when it comes to overall safety, when a predator does show up – wolf, bear, lion or even a person they don't recognize – sheep very quickly shift into a singular mindset of self-preservation. There is no "fight or flight" – it's only flight with sheep. If a predator is in the midst of the flock, the sheep with offspring don't even do anything to try to protect their young. They are only concerned with saving themselves.

Also, sheep are weak. They have absolutely no way to defend themselves, only offering a soft warm place on their wool-covered backs for a predator to sink its teeth. So when left to fend for themselves, sheep do not normally have a successful, or very extensive, run at life.

Sheep are natural followers, and often the leader is

just the first one to move. Sheep have to be led to pastures where they can graze, or else they would wander aimlessly, not even knowing where to find food.

This makes sheep highly dependent on a shepherd. Sheep struggle to survive and thrive without a shepherd. The flock forms a bond of trust with their shepherd and follows his voice without hesitation, although they still tend to panic and flee at the first sign of danger. However, a shepherd's goal is to protect the sheep, and he does whatever is necessary to keep his flock safe.

With these facts about sheep in mind, I want to suggest that when Jesus is talking about sheep in this parable, he means us. To God, humans = sheep, and he is the Shepherd. Before you get offended, and start bleating your objections, let's think about this.

We can be very fearful, extremely irrational, exceptionally selfish, and, even though we don't like to admit it, many of us are very weak. We think we are in control of our lives, but in reality we are often blindly following the example set for us by our parents, role models, or peers, without even realizing it. When we try to assert our independence and fend for ourselves, we often make a huge mess of our lives, and struggle to understand why. The truth is, we are sheep without a Shepherd,[1] and until we realize that we are solely dependent on the God who created us to give us the very breath in our lungs, we will never find our place in the flock.

This story is not about sheep. It's about you, and it's about me. The question is, what kind of sheep are you?

STRAYING

The key element in this parable is that one of the sheep has strayed away from the rest of the flock. There are many reasons this could have happened. Maybe fear caused this sheep to panic and run in the other direction. Maybe he was being bullied by the other sheep, and rejection pushed him to the outskirts of the flock. Maybe he thought the next hill looked a little greener and decided to go investigate. Or maybe he was just bored or distracted and didn't notice that the rest of the flock was moving without him. Whatever the reason, once a sheep begins to stray, it is almost impossible for him to find his way back. Remember, sheep are followers, but if there's no one to follow ... they're in deep trouble.

I have seen many examples of people who stray, intentionally or unintentionally, from God and others. Sometimes we make a conscious choice to turn down a path that leads us away from God and the relationships that could guide and protect us. This usually happens when we are hurt, rejected, or offended by someone who claimed to be a Christian, or when we experience a terrible tragedy or disappointment and wrongly blame God for what happened. We come to believe that we are better off trying to survive on our own, and we renounce God who we believe doesn't care and doesn't provide the way we think he should.

Another reason we might intentionally stray is when we get caught up in a behavior or relationship that begins to take precedence over everything else in our lives. We choose temporary pleasures over the eternal blessings that God wants to give us. The problem with this is that when we choose to satisfy our every desire in our own way, it never works. We are left feeling empty and needing more and more of that thing to give us the same amount of pleasure we first experienced. This pattern of addiction or sin leads us to feel ashamed, and we pull away from our other relationships and from God because we don't want anyone to know we are struggling.

The most common form of straying, and perhaps the most frightening, doesn't happen intentionally. Most of us gradually drift away from God and his plans for our lives without ever realizing that it is happening. We become so busy with life that we never see the warning signs or signals indicating we are no longer on course. We get so entrenched in routines, so comfortable with our habits and systems, that we stop listening for God's voice to guide us. Many times, even reading the Bible becomes so repetitious, just another thing to check off the to-do list, that the truth of God's word becomes like white noise. If we never apply what God is saying to our lives, the gap between our hearts and God grows and grows. Eventually, we stop reading the Bible, we stop going to church, we stop praying, and we start wondering if God is really there at all. It feels like he's abandoned us, but the truth is, we have strayed.

My definition of the word "stray" is to wander about without a destination or purpose. There are many times in my life that I have strayed and found myself somewhere without knowing how I ended up there. If you identify with any of the scenarios I've described, chances are that when you get really honest with yourself, you feel empty, lonely, confused, and purposeless. We will all reach a point in our lives when we feel like a sheep without a shepherd, living aimlessly, with no purpose or destination. We need to realize that this feeling comes from distancing ourselves from God.

Whether we've done this intentionally or unintentionally, we need to become more conscious of this tendency in our lives, and guard ourselves from wandering off.

Isaiah 53:6 says, "All of us, like sheep, have strayed away. We have left God's paths to follow our own." Once we realize that our own paths ultimately lead us to a place we don't want to be, then we can start to discover the heart of Jesus in this parable.

LOST IN THE WILDERNESS

If you have ever been lost, you understand the fear and feeling of separation it creates. Whether you were a small child who wandered away from mom in the grocery store, or an adult in an unfamiliar city who spent hours driving in circles, unable to locate your destination, there was probably a panic that gripped your heart the moment you realized, "I'm lost."

When I was about 7 years old, I got lost at Sea World. At first, I didn't even realize that my family was gone. My sole focus was to get as close as possible to the enormous, black killer whale. I was determined that I was going to jump on that whale's back and ride him around like *Free Willy*. In pursuit of my whale riding dreams, I drifted away, and was completely separated from my family. When I came to my senses and didn't recognize any of the faces surrounding me, I remember terror crashing over me like water spouting from the whale's blowhole.

Being lost produces incomparable fear. Everything around you looks unfamiliar and dangerous. You don't know who to trust or where to go for help. Fear paralyzes you as you start to wonder what will happen if no one finds you.

In Jesus' story, the sheep strays away and gets lost in the wilderness. Now, I think it's possible to stray just a little and still be able to find your way back, but, more often than not, you aren't aware you are straying until you look up and realize that you don't know where you are. Some people never look up and never realize they are lost, because they think they're just following their own path.

Before Jesus showed up, most people didn't know that they were living aimless, empty lives, far from what God had intended for them. When the tax collectors and notorious sinners heard Jesus' words, it stirred something in them, and suddenly their lives of sin and selfishness didn't look as appealing as what Jesus offered. The same is true for us today. We are constantly wandering, searching for the magic ingredient for happiness or success or fulfillment, and we don't realize we're lost in the wilderness, without any clue where we're supposed to be. Until we hear the Shepherd's voice, we will never find our way.

The problem with being truly lost is that you are totally dependent on someone else to find you and lead you back to where you need to be. It's like those extreme mountain skiers. They ski so far off the beaten path that if something bad happens, the only hope they have is for someone to come looking for them. That's exactly what Jesus does.

> Wouldn't you ... search for the lost one until you found it?[2] The Son of Man came to seek and save those who are lost.[3] I am the good shepherd. The good shepherd lays down his life for the sheep.[4]

Before you even knew you were lost, God was making a way

for you to get back to him. He sees every fear, every struggle, every moment of loneliness and confusion, every decision you make that takes you farther away from him – and still he pursues you. Romans 5:8 says, "God demonstrates his own love for us in this: while we were still sinners, Christ died for us" (NIV). While we were still sinners. While we were doing whatever we pleased, hating God and walking away from the safety of his love to wander the darkness and wilderness of this world, creating notoriety for ourselves in all the wrong ways – that's when Jesus came and gave his life for us, his sheep.

You are never too lost that God's love cannot reach you. He has not forgotten about you; he has not abandoned you. You could have been the ONLY person in the world, and Jesus still would have given his life to save you. He wants you to come back to the flock. He wants you to follow him. You just have to open your ears, listen for his voice, turn from the path you've been wandering and follow.

THE 99

As people have read this parable ever since it was first recorded in scripture, I'm certain that some have questioned the shepherd's common sense. *What about the 99? Why would a shepherd leave the entire flock just to go after the one sheep who was crazy enough to wander away from the safety and protection of the flock? It's just one sheep; why not let it get what it deserves for its foolish decision?*

The answer, though it may seem simple, unlocks a greater principle for us to understand. The 99 sheep left in the flock didn't need to be saved. They were safe; they had not strayed away. They were not in the wilderness alone; they had each other for support and comfort until the shepherd returned. The 99 didn't need the shepherd as urgently as the one, so he left them. First, this shows us how important each individual sheep is to the shepherd. Second, it means that the shepherd trusts the 99 sheep; he's confident that they won't wander off while he is gone.

However, in today's church (flock), many of us have these questions and offenses rising in our hearts and minds. We see someone getting extra attention from a pastor, and we start to get a weird feeling because we think that person, who has not been as good as we have, does not deserve the attention. Of course, we don't want to admit thinking this way, but we can't help feeling like we are being left behind and not getting our needs met, because this messed up person is stealing the spotlight.

Allowing ourselves to entertain thoughts like these can have two results. First, we can become needy and clingy Christians, who act out in negative ways just to gain attention. We see that people with problems get more face time with the pastors, so we start to create or magnify our own issues so we can have that one-on-one experience we think we deserve. Needy, clingy Christians can put a damper on the growth of new believers in a church. If the church is too busy shearing and feeding the sheep that are already there, they cannot focus on finding and reaching the lost ones, like Jesus commands.

Second, when we think this way, we can become judgmental, superior Christians. Much like the Pharisees to whom Jesus told this parable, we can set ourselves up on a pedestal as "the 99 righteous" looking down on the scum who strayed or aren't part of the flock. This is so far from God's heart, and we have to be careful to remember that we are not better than anyone else just because we stayed with the flock. Remember what it said in Isaiah, we ALL, like sheep, have gone astray.[5] At one point, we were all lost – and would still be lost – if not for Jesus. We cannot view the church as an exclusive club. Instead of being jealous or offended or turning our noses up when a pastor spends more time talking to a notorious sinner than to us, we should rejoice in the fact that we are already saved, and that someone else may experience that same salvation.

Jesus needs to be able to trust the 99 to follow his voice and his vision. His mission on earth was to save the lost, and once you've been found, he passes the torch to you. If you are part of the 99, then people who are lost must become as important to you as they are to Jesus.

SEARCH AND RESCUE

I am really good at losing things. I have spent countless hours searching for my keys, my phone, my wallet, or an important piece of paper. Most of the time, the item is right in front of my eyes. I don't have a lot of patience, so when I am searching for a lost object, I get increasingly frustrated and angry, which makes the entire process a miserable one. More than once, I have seen an infomercial for a product that locates your keys or wallet, and I would have dialed the number to order it, but I couldn't find my phone.

When I was sixteen, one of my most treasured possessions was my black Nike backpack. I loved this bag. It had just the right balance of style and simplicity. It was the perfect size to carry my gym clothes and school books with ease, and since I used it so much it formed perfectly to my shoulders and whatever I put inside. Most people got a new backpack every school year, but once I had this black Nike bag, I didn't need anything else. I planned on keeping it for the rest of my life. I never wanted another backpack.

One evening after a long day of school and work, I discovered that my black Nike backpack was missing. I went outside to check my car, but it wasn't there. I ransacked the entire house searching for my bag, but I couldn't find it. As I became more and more frustrated over the loss of my favorite backpack, I thought about all the places I had been that day. I knew for certain I had my black Nike backpack with me when I left school to go to work, but from there I could not fathom how it had disappeared.

I had a job at the local grocery store in my small country town. It was pretty safe, and few thefts or robberies occurred. If you left your windows down in your car in a parking lot, you could be fairly confident that no one would mess with your car or the stuff you had inside of it. This was especially true for me because I drove a rusty 1992 Chevy Lumina. It was definitely not a prime candidate for a break-in. On top of that, there was absolutely nothing of value inside my car, or inside my black Nike backpack. In my experience, stinky gym clothes and unfinished math homework don't sell too well on the black market, so why would someone have stolen it from my car (which was the only explanation I was left with by this time)?

Even at that age, I was used to misplacing or losing a lot of things, but the loss of my black Nike bag was devastating. I had lost the one and only bag that I loved. Don't think I'm exaggerating just to make a good story, either. My attachment to baggage is a very real part of my life. When I was three years old, I had a Mickey Mouse suitcase that I would take with me every time I went to my grandparents' house. As I sit here and write this book, I am still the proud owner of that Mickey Mouse suitcase. I don't let a good piece of baggage just pass through my life. When I like a bag, I keep it.

Several days passed and I had almost lost hope of ever being reunited with my precious Nike backpack, when I got a phone call from a little old lady who lived on the other side of town. She asked me if I was the owner of a black bag, and, amazed and excited, I answered yes. I wondered if maybe she was holding my bag for ransom, but I was willing to do anything to get it back.

Apparently, she had found the bag the day before next to her mailbox when she went to get her mail. She said that she had not been outside to check her mail for a few days because of the weather. It was winter in northeast Ohio, and a big snowstorm had hit right after I lost my bag. I was just glad that she had finally discovered my bag, rescued it, and was kind enough to call my phone number on the tag. We arranged that I would pick up my long lost backpack at her house the next day.

The weather was still very bad, and as a new driver I did not feel confident navigating the roads for this adventure, so I asked my dad to drive me to this lady's house. Also, it was safer to bring someone else along, because I couldn't be sure this old lady wasn't a serial killer who was going to eat me like Hansel and Gretel. The idea of being stuffed full of candy and consumed whole was really not appealing to me (although I'm kind of okay with the candy part).

When we pulled up to her house, it was obvious that she didn't leave her house often, and made no effort at snow and ice management. The driveway was a solid sheet of ice, and the walkway to the house was buried under snow. With my dad waiting and watching from the car, I made the trek to the front door and knocked. She opened the door and asked if I was Doug, and I responded eagerly that I was. This didn't seem to be enough information for her, so she made me describe exactly what my black Nike bag looked like. She obviously spent most of her time watching criminal investigation shows. Finally, satisfied with my description, she revealed my long-awaited prize, and handed the black Nike backpack to me with just one warning, "Now, son, it's got a funny odor to it."

The odor, I immediately concluded, was urine. So, not only had an individual pillaged my car and stolen my backpack, but upon finding it contained nothing of value, decided it was necessary to urinate in it before throwing it on the side of the road.

I was standing in some random old lady's living room, holding a pee-stained backpack, but I loved that bag too much to get rid of it just because of a little bit of urine. I told the lady I would just throw it in the washer, thanked her, and quickly exited through the front door. Glowing with delight over recovering my beloved backpack, I couldn't wait to show my father that I had found what was lost. So, in the style of *The Lion King*, I raised the bag high above my head in triumph, both arms stretched towards the sky, and gave a warrior cry as if to announce my firstborn child to the world. But my jubilation was cut short and suddenly I was lying flat on my back, writhing in pain, with the urine-soaked bag directly on my face.

As I pulled the bag off my face, I registered that the ice rink driveway had taken me down hard. While I lay there moaning and thinking I had a concussion, I began to call to my dad (who was still sitting comfortably in the car) for help. My dad's "help" amounted to him rolling down the window and, through his laughter, saying, "Ahh, you'll be all right. Get up." Thanks, Dad. After two minutes of struggling to stand and walk on the frozen tundra, I made it back to the car, still clutching my backpack that I had now suffered and bent over backwards (almost literally) to get back.

I have not just told you this story just so you can laugh at my stupidity; I am also trying to help you understand my point. When you lose something that is important to you, it doesn't matter how hard the journey is (or how many smells or spills you have to endure), because when you finally recover what you lost, everything was worth it. I didn't let anything keep me from retrieving my black Nike backpack, and I still have that bag (right next to my Mickey Mouse luggage) to this day. Having my favorite bag back was so worth all of the hassle I endured to get it.

If I felt that way about finding a backpack, imagine how much more God feels that way about you, his creation. If you are lost or wandering, know this: You are worth the search. Maybe you have strayed away from the flock, or maybe you were never part of the flock to begin with. Either way, God cares about you right where you are and he has gone to great lengths to save you. He gave his only Son, who sacrificed his life in place of yours. Jesus paid the penalty for our sin and died a horrible death so that we could have life. Falling on some ice for a bag pales in comparison.

After Jesus defeated death, he came back and asked us to carry on his mission of seeking and saving the lost. How can we say no when we realize what he has done to save us? Even though it is a difficult mission, full of pain, rejection, and sorrow, we cannot stop searching. When you reach one lost person, you will realize one thing: It's worth it.

CHAPTER EIGHT

REFLECTION & APPLICATION

Do you feel far from God? Have you strayed, intentionally or unintentionally?

Have you ever lost something or someone and would go to any lengths to get it back?

Have you ever felt jealous that another person got more attention than they deserved?

CHAPTER NINE

JOYFUL, JOYFUL

"*And then you would* JOYFULLY CARRY IT HOME *on your* SHOULDERS."

Luke 15:5

Have you ever watched a little kid try to pick up a sibling or an animal? It's hilarious. They grab on wherever they can and struggle awkwardly to lift their victim inches off the floor, holding as tightly as possible. Most commonly, this results in the sibling getting strangled or the dog getting its tail trampled or everyone involved falling to the ground. This is sometimes painful to watch, if you can imagine how it would feel to be in a toddler death grip. It is obvious that they have no idea how to carry something, which is understandable since they are only 2 or 3 years old, but they don't know that. They're usually beaming with pride at their accomplishment (until the inevitable injury of one party or the other occurs).

Every once in a while, I serve in "Mini Movement," the kids ministry at our church. Hanging out with children five and under, and watching them explore motor skills for the first time can be very entertaining. I love seeing little kids pick up something as everyone cheers, claps, and shouts encouragement. They hold the object in the air and smile from ear to ear. Even though it's awkward and they can't carry very much very far, children are so joyful when they succeed because of the positive response that they get from their actions.

In this scripture, Jesus conveys this idea of the shepherd *joyfully* carrying a sheep on his shoulders. Just like the child who joyfully picks up a toy for the first time, the shepherd is full of joy when he finds and rescues his sheep. He isn't irritated, thinking, "This dumb sheep wandered off, got himself stuck and injured, and now I have to carry him back. I should make him walk to teach him a lesson." Rather, he is so excited to have found his lost sheep, he doesn't hesitate to lift it up. He is happy to carry it.

When I think about carrying something on my shoulders, I don't normally associate it with joy. Especially if it's a sheep. Holding something that is moving and unstable, constantly redistributing its weight, is not an easy process. I have actually never equated joy with back-breaking labor at any time in my life. This is not a little lamb we're talking about, this is a full grown sheep weighing anywhere from 150 to 200 pounds. Plus, it has been wandering around in the wilderness for who knows how long, so it is probably extremely filthy and stinky (more than usual), not to mention it has to be a significant distance away from the rest of the flock to be considered lost. Personally, I would compare the long walk with a heavy, smelly, dirty sheep on your shoulders to Frodo taking the ring of power to Mordor (*Lord of the Rings* nerd alert). With every step your burden gets heavier and heavier, it feels like your journey will never end, and you smell like an Orc by the time you reach your destination.

But this is not how Jesus described it.

He says "you would *joyfully* carry it home on your shoulders." In the Greek, the word translated "joyfully" means that he is continually rejoicing. He is rejoicing when he finds the sheep, he's rejoicing as he hoists it up on his shoulders, he's rejoicing as he carries it all the way home.

What we have to understand is that when the shepherd finally finds that one lost sheep, the joy of finding it outweighs the hardship of carrying it. The shepherd doesn't care how dirty or how heavy the sheep may be, he is simply overjoyed that he has found the one for whom he searched so long. Saving the lost sheep was the shepherd's goal the entire time, and in reaching that goal, the shepherd is filled with so much joy he doesn't notice how messed up the sheep is or how difficult the journey will be.

Hebrews 12:2 says that Jesus endured the cross, disregarding its shame, "because of the joy awaiting him." I believe part of that joy was being reunited with us, the people he loved. He was willing to go through hell (literally) to save us, but he knew that once it was finished, he wouldn't be able to contain his joy. It doesn't matter how broken or jacked up or dirty or heavy we are when he finds us, Jesus is ecstatic to pick us up and carry us home.

I think that being carried on his shoulders is an interesting picture, because we are not only being fully supported by him, but we are close enough to hear his voice. The journey alone with Jesus as he is carrying you back to the flock is an important time, because he is talking to you, rejoicing over you, and you are learning to recognize his voice, so that when you get back and get all cleaned up, you don't stray again.

How we respond to this time of being carried is important.

I've had to pick up a few animals (mostly dogs and cats) and, in my experience, most animals who weigh over 20 pounds do not like being carried. They are comfortable with all four paws on the ground and if you are going to attempt otherwise, there's going to be a struggle.

My main experience with animal handling has been with my dog, Gryffindor, or Gryff for short (yes, it's from *Harry Potter* ... don't judge me). My wife and I got Gryff as a puppy a few months after we were married. He was so tiny when we got him, we could hold him in one hand. Now, however, Gryff weighs over 100 pounds with a thick, muscular body and very little fat. We think he's a boxer/lab/pit/dane mix, but we're not sure. Either way, he is beautiful – sleek black with white markings; the definition of a big, strong dog.

When Gryff was still very small, we lived in a rented condo with nice white carpeting. It was a challenge to keep this place clean with a brand new puppy, so at about three months old, I felt it was necessary to introduce Gryff to the concept of bathing. My plan was to bathe him in the kitchen sink, like some people would do with a human baby, so I picked him up with ease, and put him under the faucet. In my lack of experience with babies and puppies, I failed to realize that the water was way too hot. From Gryff's perspective, I imagine he thought he was getting cooked, so he freaked out. He started yelping and biting with his tiny dagger teeth. Puppy teeth are brutal because they haven't been rounded off yet from chewing on bones and food. So as Gryff was being scalded and writhing around, my hands were being pierced with twenty tiny daggers, and I got angry. Yes, my red hair often has a temper to match. Even after I changed the temperature of the water, Gryff wouldn't stop freaking out, and my frustration was mounting. I finally grabbed him and shoved him into submission, which I realize was not the proper reaction, but the biting pushed me over the edge. Side note: If you are part of PETA, please know that this was an isolated incident. I do not mistreat animals; I love dogs, and Gryff is very healthy and happy.

However, the traumatic experience that Gryff and I endured together at that young and fragile stage of his life has caused some lasting damage. To this day, Gryff is terrified of getting a bath. He isn't afraid of water, because when we go to the local lake, he jumps right in and swims like a pro. Gryff loves water, but he hates taking a bath. He's gotten so smart that he won't even risk entering a bathroom. Even if there was a massive steak covered with peanut butter sitting on the edge of the tub, he wouldn't go near it.

When Gryff's need for a bath becomes unavoidable, it takes a lot of maneuvering and patience on my end to make it happen. After I have coaxed him down the hallway as far as he will go, I have to pick up his 100-pound body and carry him the rest of the way into the bathroom. I then have to lift him up over the side of the tub, which is not all that easy since he is only about 70 pounds lighter than I am. Not only is he heavy, but the whole time he seems to be fighting for his life – his muscles are tensed, his legs are flailing, his paws are scratching at everything hoping to find traction somewhere to keep himself out of the tub.

I try to calm him, saying things like, "Gryffindor, you are a big, brave, strong dog! This water will not hurt you!" I even find myself apologizing to him for the trauma that I caused him all those years ago. Encouragement of "good boy" and "you're okay" and endless petting seem to have no effect on him. He fights throughout the entire process, and I end up needing a shower and massage after the acrobatics of Gryffindor's bath time.

I wonder how many times we fight and struggle when God is trying to carry us. Just like Gryff, we have mental barriers when it comes to trusting our Master. Because of traumatic experiences in our past, or all the issues that going through the wilderness alone produced in our lives, we often resist God when he tries to pick us up and save us. We blame God for the mud that we have walked through, and the dirt that is caked over our hearts and minds because of the choices that we made. We raise the barriers, and reinforce them, because we think that God allowed terrible things to happen to us because he doesn't love us or care about us. We need to begin to learn how to lower these mental barriers, and stop resisting God when he is trying to carry us to a place where he can clean us up.

At some point in our lives every one of us needs to be carried. Now, as a grown man, I wouldn't be partial to the idea of someone picking me up, but allowing ourselves to be carried is more a posture of our heart and mind than it is a physical position. The Bible is full of encouragement for us to trust God, but it's hard to do. We have to believe that God is not going to drop us, that he knows where to go better than we do. I Peter 5:6-7 says, "Humble yourselves under the mighty power of God, and at the right time he will lift you up in honor. Give all your worries and cares to God, for he cares about you."

Being carried requires that we humble ourselves, forgetting the pride that made us think we could make it on our own. Only then will we discover "the joys of those who trust the Lord"[1] and be able to rejoice with our Shepherd when he finds and carries us and others.

———————

There are two challenges I want to offer to you.

First, I want to address those of you who need to be carried in from the wilderness, and you're fighting it, like Gryff going for his bath. You are kicking and screaming and doing anything you can to avoid going on this journey with God. You don't like the feeling of not being in control, not having both feet on solid ground. The problem is, where you were standing before was not solid ground, and God wants to take you to a place that is. He is the only firm foundation that we can build our lives on. He is the only one who understands where you've been and what you need to move forward. My challenge to you is this: Stop fighting and simply trust. "For the word of the Lord holds true, and we can trust everything he does."[2]

Second, God may be asking you to help carry someone else right now. Maybe there is someone you have been trying to help find God, or someone you have been praying would find God for a long time, but they are fighting him and you. You might feel exhausted and ready to give up, but my challenge is simply: Don't. Galatians 6:2-3 urges us to "share each other's burdens, and in this way obey the law of Christ. If you think you are too important to help someone, you are only fooling yourself. You are not that important." Even though it's hard, and heavy, and you might get kicked in the back of the head, God wants us to carry each other's burdens. Remember to have a joyful spirit in the midst of the struggle, because eventually you will be able to rejoice with them when they are back where they belong.

CHAPTER NINE

REFLECTION & APPLICATION

Are you lacking joy? Read and pray Psalm 51:12-13.

Do you need to humble yourself and let God to carry you?

Read Galatians 6.
Do you need to help or carry someone? Who has a burden that you could share?

CHAPTER TEN

THE GOSPEL OF CELEBRATION

> **"WHEN YOU ARRIVED, YOU WOULD** *call together your friends and neighbors* **TO REJOICE WITH YOU BECAUSE YOUR LOST SHEEP WAS FOUND.** *In the same way, heaven will be happier over* **ONE LOST SINNER WHO RETURNS TO GOD THAN OVER 99 OTHERS** *who are righteous* **AND HAVEN'T STRAYED AWAY!"**
>
> *Luke 15:6-7*

I love to throw parties. I love to have a good time. Getting people together to be entertained, laugh, and make memories makes me come alive. Before Christ, I loved to party, and now, living as a Jesus follower, I have learned how to have an amazing time and party without sinning or doing things I regret the next day. I have learned how to be really good at celebrating. God is a God of celebration, and he loves to party with us.

Too many times I think we are against celebrating

for fear of where it will lead us, but God has a different perspective. All throughout the Bible, God challenges his people to celebrate and rejoice. He wants us to celebrate his goodness, have a good time together, and rejoice in the good things that he is doing. He even set up feasts for the people of Israel to celebrate each month and year, so they would not forget to party and enjoy what God had done for them. We may not follow the traditions of the Jewish calendar, but I believe that God wants us to gather together every once in a while and actually celebrate, not just in a worship service, but by throwing a party.

When my wife, Stephanie, was turning 25 years old, I thought it would be a great idea to have a surprise party for her. If you knew my wife, you would know that "surprise," "party," and "Stephanie" are three words she would never want to hear in the same sentence. But we were still dating at this time, and I loved parties so much that it was hard to believe she wouldn't appreciate this gesture. At that time, she was in a play with performances that lasted late into the night, which created the perfect opportunity to set up the surprise inside my efficiency apartment. Now, when I say "efficiency" I mean it could comfortably accommodate about ten people, if I used the shower as a place for people to stand. Somehow, I crammed 25 of our closest friends and family into my apartment. After borrowing furniture and breaking fire code, everyone was positioned for the birthday surprise.

At the same time, Stephanie was just finishing her show that night and planning to stop by to see me before heading home. Stage performers go through a lot of makeup, energy, and sweat for just one performance, and afterwards they normally just strip off the makeup and throw their

THE GOSPEL JESUS INTENDED

hair up and want to go collapse at home. Stephanie was in that state of mind and exhaustion when she showed up to the apartment. When she walked in the door and everyone shouted "Surprise!" she was stunned.

But wait, the best part of the story is still to come. My other stroke of brilliance for this party was to have Stephanie, who also worked as a cake decorator for a bakery, create her own birthday cake without knowing it. She had shown me a picture of a cake she had decorated previously and was proud of, so I tried to relay to her coworker for her to design that same cake. Something got lost in translation, and instead of decorating a cake she loved and was proud of, Stephanie ended up decorating the cake according to her coworker's confusing description, and hated everything about it. So, as she was getting over her initial shock at this unexpected birthday party and the amount of people crammed into my apartment, the crowd parted and she saw the cake that she had decorated sitting on the table. This was too much for her to handle, and she exclaimed, in embarrassment and disbelief, how much she hated making the cake and how hideous she thought it was (it really wasn't that bad). An awkward silence fell over the room. I, being the happy party guy, quickly said, "Who cares what it looks like? Let's just eat it!" Everyone seemed to have a good time after that, and even Stephanie calmed down and enjoyed herself, but I haven't attempted to throw any surprise parties since then. Looking back, I learned that despite my best efforts for throwing an awesome party, things don't always go the way that I plan, and not everyone values partying as much as I do.

My wife barely wanted to celebrate her own birthday with other people, but in the scripture we have been studying,

Jesus tells us that he would call together all his friends and neighbors to celebrate finding a lost sheep. This sounds like me – any excuse to throw a party. But Jesus is making it clear to the notorious sinners, tax collectors, and Pharisees (and to us) that celebrating isn't optional. It should be your first priority, your natural response to the lost being found.

Why is partying and celebrating such a big deal to Jesus? Why would he intentionally choose to teach this principle at the end of this parable? After much thought, I want to offer three reasons as to why Jesus and all of heaven make celebrating a priority.

LOST AND FOUND

There is a natural excitement that comes with recovering and reclaiming what is lost. You remember the story from chapter 8 about my black Nike backpack – the devastation I felt in losing it and the elation that came with finding it again. Before something is found, we are in panic mode, worried that whatever is lost will never be found again. As fear rises inside of us, our minds race, imagining all of the worst possible outcomes for the situation. We are very good at assuming the worst instead of expecting the best.

Jesus understood the intensity of the emotions that we feel when something is lost, so in teaching celebration, he is teaching us that we should have an equally intense emotional response when something is found. We need to encourage and cultivate this excitement, lest we forget how God has designed us.

The Bible tells us that we were created in God's image.[1] Our inclination to rejoice over things being found, saved, or restored is because God rejoices over those same things. Jesus made it very clear that there is rejoicing and celebration that happens in heaven when even *one* sinner returns to God. If we can get excited over being reunited with our earthly belongings (like my Nike bag), imagine how much more thrilled our Heavenly Father is over being reunited with the people he created, his children! God wants us to be just as excited as he is about lost ones finding where they belong. So why aren't we?

I fear that a lot of us feel that we are not allowed to share in the emotions of God like I have just described. We can have this "woe is me" mentality that causes us to believe we have to be miserable and that we don't deserve to celebrate or be happy. Many of us struggle with feelings of insufficiency and insignificance. We've been told we are not good enough – that we need to do more or be more or have more – so many times that we believe the lie. We live defeated lives and never accomplish the purposes God has intended for us. In our spiritual lives, we may feel disqualified and unworthy because of our sin. We can be "saved" and still think that we are sinners who have to somehow pay for our sins by struggling and despairing through life. This is not true!

Jesus has already paid the price and canceled the debt we owed. You were once lost but now you are found; you were in bondage but now you are free; you were a sinner but now you're a new creation. Repentance isn't just asking for forgiveness; it is turning from the way you've been living and the way you've been thinking, and turning towards God's ways. It is changing the way you think about God, yourself, and others. God wants to pull us out of the negative mindset that we aren't good enough. He makes us good enough and he wants us to experience the good things he has for us.[2] True, we do not deserve the life and joy of God, but because of his grace and mercy, God offers us an open invitation to experience the abundant life that comes from knowing him. If that's not a reason to celebrate, I don't know what is.

God wants us to party, and he wants us to enjoy life with him. God created us in his image so that we could feel the same degree of emotion that he feels when he is celebrating. It's time for us to start being the people that God intended us to be. It's time to start partying.

SHARED VICTORY

When I was starting out in ministry as a youth pastor, I had one volunteer named Chris who was an extremely hard worker and a great role model for our students. He was a unique guy and didn't care about being cool, which made him more cool. Everyone loved to be around him, and his commitment and character made me want to bless him any chance I could. I knew that Chris was struggling to put gas in his car. He only worked a minimum wage job and volunteered the rest of his time doing youth outreach and ministry. One day when I was filling up my gas tank, I felt a tug on my heart from God to bless Chris and fill his tank as well. Sometimes, though, trying to bless someone can be a bit uncomfortable, especially for guys like us who were close in age – at that time in our early 20s. I wanted to work it out so he didn't know the blessing was coming from me. I didn't want any recognition; I just wanted him to be blessed.

I went to the clerk at the gas station and told her that I had a friend I wanted to bless with some gas, but that I didn't want him to know I did it. I asked her if she would be a part of my scheme, and she gladly accepted. My plan went as follows: I was going to call my buddy Chris and tell him that the gas station was giving away $20 of free gas if you went up to the clerk and politely asked, "May I have some free gas, please?" The clerk would then respond, "Yes, you may," and give him the $20 of free gas, which I had already paid for. I told the clerk what Chris looked like, left my $20, and set out to make the call. I felt confident that this was a good plan.

I called Chris and told him the most amazing giveaway was happening at the gas station that was just down the street from his house. He let me know that I had better not be pranking him, because his tank was on empty and he might not even make it back home if he drove to the gas station and the deal wasn't for real. I assured him I wasn't joking and I elaborated a little more, saying he needed to hurry because the deal was only lasting for 10 more minutes. After reassuring him multiple times, Chris was on his way to the gas station to get his free gas.

I waited until he pulled into the parking lot, just so I could remind him the exact words he needed to say, but after my reminder I took off. I left the parking lot chuckling because the situation was funny, and ridiculous even, but I was accomplishing my goal of tangibly blessing Chris. He was supposed to meet me at my office right after filling up, but time passed and he still hadn't arrived, so I decided to give him a call. I asked where he was, but I could hardly understand what he was saying because he was so excited.

He exclaimed that I had indeed not been pranking him, and that he had been hooked up with $20 of free gas. He went on to say that he went around to random strangers at all the pumps at the gas station, and told them what they needed to say to the clerk to get hooked up with free gas as well. In that moment, I got that sick feeling in my stomach once again (just like I had sitting on the back of the bus in seventh grade, in chapter one). That wasn't all. Chris had called his sister and cousins, and they were on their way to get their free gas. He was so excited to tell everyone the good news about the free gas.

I had to come clean. I had to tell him what I had done, and that I was just trying to bless him without him knowing. I had to tell him that the entire thing was a set up, and that he was the only one who would be receiving free gas that day. It was silent on the other end of the phone, and then Chris said, "Dude, thank you so much, but I need to get off the phone and call some people and tell them not to come here."

As he hung up the phone, I imagined riots breaking out at this gas station, and the clerk who had helped me with my plan being burned at the stake because she couldn't deliver on the free gas that was promised. I kept thinking to myself what an idiot I had just been. Chris had responded like we all should at finding something we didn't expect or deserve. To him, finding free gas was amazing and worth celebrating. He could not wait to share it with everyone possible.

The second reason we need to celebrate is because God knows that when we share victory with others, it gives them strength and hope. When you call together your friends and neighbors to rejoice with you, they get to see just how good your victory is and be inspired that perhaps they can experience the same victory in their own lives.

Sharing victory can multiply victory.

One of the core values that I have worked to establish in my church is based around this reason for celebrating. I have set the standard at all of our campuses that the platform communicator (main speaker) stands at the main doors after the worship experience, shaking hands and talking with people on their way out. This used to be very common in church culture many years ago. The preacher would finish the message and walk straight out to the doors to thank everyone for attending as they made their way out of the church. This concept has been almost completely eradicated in today's church. Now we have "superstar" pastors who require entourages and body guards. These pastors come across as being so unattainable that it is unthinkable for them to stand and shake each person's hand. If they're not careful, they can be very disconnected from the sheep they are leading.

One catchphrase I love to say is, "a good shepherd should stink like his sheep." I believe I should be willing to get stinky and dirty with the sheep that I am leading. I do this by greeting them at the doors, talking with them, remembering their names, and even spending time with them at the cost of my own personal schedule sometimes. In doing this, I believe that people are able to connect with me and understand that I am an ordinary person just like them. Through my transparency and sincerity, I am actually sharing my victory with them. Even though I may be ordinary, I serve an extraordinary God who has used me in extraordinary ways, and I want them to know that. With simple acts, people can be moved to reach for their own victory, realizing that *if God can do this with Doug, he can do it with me.* The end goal is that they are inspired to leave their safety net (or the

99) and pursue that one person in their lives who has strayed away.

This mentality may be very different than anything that you have ever thought about before, but it has really defined my life. I have always done things differently. I'm not afraid to leave the safety of the pack to do things that people told me were impossible. God has been faithful to make a way where there was no way. He has allowed me to return from the wilderness time and time again, carrying the lost sheep over my shoulders. When I share these victories with others, it's not to celebrate me, it is to celebrate God, and what he can do with a notorious sinner like me. Revelation 12:11 (NIV) says, "They triumphed over [the devil] by the blood of the Lamb and by the word of their testimony." Our testimonies are powerful. When we share the things that Jesus has done and is doing in our lives and the lives of others, we bring glory to God and achieve victory over our struggles, as well as giving hope for victory to those around us.

This principle has been modeled on one of the biggest platform in sports. Russell Wilson was always an undersized football player. Growing up, everyone told him that he was too small, too skinny, and many people early in his life encouraged him to play baseball instead of football. Russell's desire, though, was to play football and to be the best. So he pursued his dream and was eventually drafted into the National Football League for the 2012-2103 season.

On average, NFL quarterbacks measure at 6'3" tall. Russell Wilson's Seattle Seahawks player sheet shows that he is only about 5'11" (and I think they add a couple of inches and pounds to make players seem bigger than they are). The lineman that play in the NFL average 6'5" tall, and many of them are 300 pounds. So, in the NFL, Russell is lining up across from guys who are almost a foot taller than him, and heavy enough to pancake him to the turf at any point. Except for his extreme conditioning and physical prowess (which I lack), this would be almost like ME, the vertically challenged ginger, lining up to play. However, this did not stop Russell Wilson from leading his team through an incredible season, and ultimately winning Super Bowl XLVIII.

In his post game interview, Russell talked about a lesson that his father taught him from a very early age. His father always used to ask him, "Why not you, Russell? Why not you?" It was this question that drove him to victory in the country's biggest sporting event, even though everyone around him said he would never make it. He made a decision that if someone had to win, it should be him. Why not? He lived his life in a way that set him up for celebration, and every victory he obtained was contagious. Before competing in the Super Bowl, he said to his teammates, "Why not us?" And they won.

As we learn to celebrate with others, sharing our victories with them and rejoicing when they share their victories with us, we can spur each other on with this question. Remember, shared victory is multiplied victory. So, why not you? God is looking for someone to change your generation, someone who will leave the 99 and go after the lost one – why not you? There are victories waiting to be had all around us, if we will trust God and approach him with this attitude: "If you're going to use someone, why not me?"

DYING TO ME

A third reason I believe we need to party is because of humility. Before you say this doesn't make sense and stop reading, hear me out. In *Mere Christianity*, C.S. Lewis says, "True humility is not thinking less of yourself. It is thinking of yourself less."[3] Think about a time when you have thrown a party. Didn't you spend hours planning and preparing, and what did you have to do afterwards? Yeah, clean up. If you throw a party, it's rarely for your own benefit; it benefits the other people who come to the party. So when we choose to celebrate, and have joy, and give thanks for the lost being found, we are learning to think less of ourselves, and focus more on others and how we can bring more glory to God.

John 3:30 says, "He [Jesus] must become greater and greater, and I must become less and less." Humility is dying to ourselves. Humility is us becoming less so that Jesus can become more and more in our lives. Whether we are the shepherd leaving the flock to search for the one, or we are the lost sheep who is being carried back, either way, we are dying to ourselves and becoming more like Jesus. Sacrificing your own time and efforts to go after the one requires humility. Allowing yourself, as one who is lost and needs saving, to be carried on someone else's shoulders is humbling. What we are really celebrating in this process is that we are becoming more like Jesus.

Whether we are turning to God for the first time, or we are reaching out to a lost person, we are dying to ourselves and coming alive in Christ. In dying to ourselves, we get over our pride and begin to do what Jesus' gospel intended for us to do.

"If any of you wants to be my follower, you must turn from your selfish ways, take up your cross daily, and follow me."[4]

Jesus' gospel is not about comfort or conformity; it's about compassion and celebration. It's about a shepherd coming after the sheep he loves so much, and saving them when they didn't deserve it. The gospel Jesus intended is such good news, but it's not easy. However, the Bible tells us we can rejoice and even boast when we run into problems and trials, and we can rejoice and boast because Jesus has made us right with God.[5]

A friend of mine, who pastors a church in Columbus, Ohio, said, "The world parties to forget, but we party to remember." If you think about it, it's a very true statement. People who do not have Christ party so they can forget how miserable their lives are. They push themselves to a state of mind where they don't have to deal with the hurts and heartaches of life, at least until the next morning. They are out in the wilderness, and, even though they may be partying alongside of others just like them, in reality, they are alone. They are separated from God, observing an endless cycle of temporary pleasures to numb their pain.

As Christ followers, we party to remember what God has done in and through our lives. We party to remember that it's not about us and it's all about Jesus. We celebrate the fact that he has redeemed us and given us a purpose for our lives. One of my goals for even writing this book is to motivate us, as Christ followers, to get fired up about truly living this gospel that Jesus intended.

We actually have an obligation to celebrate and make a big deal about what God is doing, so that those who come after us don't forget. When we party to remember, we make markers in our lives that we can come back to later in life to remind us of who God is and what he has done. When we party to remember, we make it clear to others that partying was God's idea in the first place.

CHAPTER TEN

REFLECTION & APPLICATION

What is one thing God has done in your life that you can celebrate?

How can you party to remember?

Is it possible to deny yourself (Luke 9:23) and still enjoy the journey and love the life God has given you?

Share your story with someone. Be transparent with your testimony – your struggles can give you compassion for others and your victories can inspire others to overcome their struggles.

CHAPTER ELEVEN

THE CHALLENGE

I AM SO HAPPY
YOU MADE IT THIS FAR.
Don't quit now. THIS IS
THE LAST CHAPTER
but your challenge doesn't end here.

As you have read this book, I hope it has helped to change your perspective about Jesus' intentions towards us as his sheep and the mission he intended for us as his disciples. However, you may be looking around at the modern Christian culture and wondering how we could have strayed so far from the gospel Jesus intended. Why are so many people who claim to be followers of Christ living without compassion, without celebration, and without any cost to their comfort?

We've talked about being notorious, and the truth is most Christians today are known for being judgmental and hypocritical, preaching a gospel of prosperity and self-fulfillment. Why do so many seem to be missing the point?

Even as I'm writing this, I have had to ask myself if I am really living the way Jesus intended. There is a definite inconsistency between the simple, straightforward principles that Jesus sets up in the parable of the lost sheep, and throughout the gospels, and the way most of us are living.

I want to share two reasons that I believe keep us from following the example Jesus set and fulfilling God's purpose for our lives.

SPIRITUAL INBREEDING

The first issue is what I call "spiritual inbreeding." I realize that may sound really weird to you (and it probably is weird), but it is a term I use to describe what I have observed in some modern churches. Let me explain.

In the natural world, inbreeding is when members of the same family or people who are closely related reproduce and have children together, often over several generations. The longer this takes place, the more negative side effects occur. The results of inbreeding include high risk for genetic disorders (such as mental retardation), diseases, and a much higher infant mortality rate. It's not good.

Spiritual inbreeding, as I define it, begins to take place when churches and church leaders stop looking outside the four walls of the church. Whether they're afraid of being contaminated by the world or they're too busy keeping their flock happy, they stop reaching out to people who don't already fit into their group. They only associate with others who are like them, and if this goes on for too long, they begin to produce people with spiritual handicaps and defects.

Imagine a family who barricaded their home from

outside influence, and never left or allowed anyone else to enter their circle. They taught their children they can only befriend and marry each other. They reproduced only with other members of the family and those children grew up learning that the only real part of the world was the four walls they live behind. As much as that may disturb you, you know you would still watch the reality show (at least, I know I would). Over time, you would observe habits and behaviors that would probably freak you out. With no connection to the outside world, the family would never be exposed to new ideas or new technology. Everything this family did would be an attempt to continue to successfully coexist and keep anything that might threaten their way of life away. No matter how weird or foreign or bizarre their lifestyle seemed to you, it would be normal to them.

Now imagine that family is a local church. Ten or twenty or a hundred years ago, they were living out the gospel, going after the lost, and God blessed them. But then, whether because they got worn out or taken advantage of too many times or caught up in managing the organization they built or the world started to get too crazy, they decided it would be easier to focus on those already inside the church rather than dealing with the problems and mess that comes with "sinners." Then, they become consumed with keeping themselves happy and entertained and spiritually fed. They teach their children they should only befriend and marry others in the church. They develop habits and traditions and language that only makes sense to them. Over time, spiritual deformities and handicaps are born out of this environment.

I'm not talking about a cult here – spiritual inbreeding can happen in a normal church. Often, it is so subtle they don't even realize they've gone down this path until years later they look up and wonder why their church is dying. The problem is that instead of realizing they have strayed away from a huge part of the gospel, they often try to recreate or imitate the excitement of a church that is following Jesus' commands. They end up swinging from the chandeliers and instead of reaching the lost, they repel the lost (who think they're crazy). They produce spiritually handicapped Christians – Christians who boycott the media but think it's okay to gossip, who quote "love your neighbor as yourself" but have never met their actual neighbors, who preach salvation but never really change. They act religious, but they have mutated the message of the gospel and are missing the heart of Jesus. They appear to be godly, but they reject the power that could actually make them so. The Bible warns us to stay away from these kind of people.[1] Spiritual inbreeding in a church inhibits the fulfillment of Jesus' purpose for his church.

MIRROR, MIRROR

The second issue I want to discuss brings this from a corporate to a more personal level. I think we often struggle with thinking that Jesus' call to seek and save the lost is someone else's mission. It's easy to think that the great commission was meant for "the church" or our pastor and to ignore our individual responsibility. Why is it so easy? Because we are naturally self-centered. But just like a church who focuses only on itself will breed dysfunction, if we stay focused only on ourselves for too long, we will eventually become miserable.

Try this: Go into a room by yourself and lock the door if you can. Strip down butt naked and stare at yourself in a mirror for five solid minutes. During that five minutes, try to mentally record or write down every single thought you have as you look at yourself.

How many of those thoughts were negative? It is interesting to note the things that even people with really great bodies point out. They don't like their calf muscle, or their forehead is too wide. These people complain about a body that I would consider sacrificing my firstborn to have (just kidding). But seriously, they focus on an ear lobe that is too long or a pinky toe that protrudes at a weird angle. It seems ridiculous, but even people who have what most would consider perfect bodies are able to point out defects if they look for long enough. I know I would have no trouble finding things I don't like about my physical appearance. My list would go on and on and on.

The same thing can happen spiritually. Now, I'm not saying we should never be introspective and evaluate our minds and hearts, but I believe we have allowed ourselves to be influenced by a culture that says "it's all about me" and "have it your way" rather than really listening to God's word. Too many Christians live with this mirror, mirror mindset – focused entirely on themselves – and the more they look, the less they like. Their pursuit of God revolves solely around their needs, their struggles, their flaws, their desires. They never think that they were created *for* God,[2] but act like God is a genie in a bottle, who exists to grant their wishes and fix all their problems.

Self-absorbed Christians often do this thing we like to call "church-hopping," moving from church to church, trying to find a place that makes them feel better about themselves. It's like saying you want to be in a healthy relationship, but dating someone new every week. When the hot pink Hollywood love fades, you break off the relationship and start hunting down the next new romance. Church-hoppers are never satisfied. When the new car smell wears off, there will be something they don't like, someone will offend them, they will feel like their needs aren't being met or say they aren't being "fed," and they will hop to the next church to try to find what they lack.

My friend Landon says, "Mature people don't need to be fed, they feed themselves." And it's true. There is no church that can fix your problems or fulfill your needs. Only God can do that, but even he will have a hard time working with you if you can't get past looking in the mirror. If your main concern is your personal spiritual growth, or finding a church where you can be "fed," you are missing the point of the gospel. Remember, the more you look, the less you like. If you stay focused on yourself, you will remain immature, ineffective, and unhappy. But if you fix your eyes on Jesus, you'll be able to persevere, mature, and discover a joy that only comes from sacrificing yourself for others.[3]

There comes a point when you have to realize, THIS IS NOT ABOUT YOU. Yes, God loves you and chose you, but not only for your sake. He rescued you so that you can rescue others. God placed you on this planet, in this generation, in the exact place you're located because he wants you to be a part of reaching the lost around you. You'll never be perfect, but God will still use you. You will never find a perfect church, but you can find one that is committed to living out the great commission and partner with them to reach the lost.

THE GOSPEL JESUS INTENDED

Right after I made a decision to follow Jesus, I ran into an old friend who knew me from high school. Steve was a great football player, and we used to work out together, party together, and have a great time. I was a very new and very raw Christ follower at that time, and I didn't really know anything outside of the fact that Jesus had changed me and I wanted to tell everyone. So when I ran into Steve in the middle of the parking lot of a local store, he instantly noticed that there was something different about me, and in that moment I spewed out everything that I knew about the gospel to him. If I had to guess, I'd say probably about 80% of what I said that day was not biblically accurate, but I didn't know or care. I told Steve that Jesus loved me and had saved me, and that Jesus loved him and wanted to save him, too.

Remember, Steve knew me before Jesus – when I was notorious for throwing parties, causing trouble, and getting caught. He was moved by the fact that my new passion for Jesus was so strong. In that parking lot, we prayed together that Jesus would do the same thing in Steve that he had done in me. From that moment, we became accountability buddies, and we began experiencing our new faith in Jesus together. We did our best to support each other, and we made great leaps and bounds in our relationships with Jesus, even though we still made plenty of mistakes.

––––––––––––

What I love about that experience in my life is that God was able to use a kid like me, who was two weeks into his faith, to reach another kid, who in turn reached another kid, and so on. The gospel of Jesus was advanced in incredible ways simply because I was doing what Luke 15 instructs us to do. I didn't even know I was doing it, but I left the protection of the flock to go after my one friend who was still lost in the wilderness. I took my eyes off of my own needs, and I focused on his.

I think that sometimes we forget what it was like when we first encountered Jesus – the love, the peace, the joy that flooded our hearts; the feeling of being made new. It's contagious. Often in those early days, we make the most impact on others because we are so passionate about sharing what God has done in our lives. But we need to remember that Jesus didn't put a time limit on his commands. He didn't say, "Go make disciples until you don't feel like doing it anymore" or "Take up your cross and follow me for a few days to prove you are serious, and then you don't need to carry it anymore."

As I hope has been made clear throughout this book, the gospel Jesus intended is not one of comfort or contentment. It's not about your happiness. It's not about what you want. It's not about you at all. It's about Jesus. It's about knowing him and making him known to others.

The good news isn't that we can live a cushy, comfortable, complacent life. The good news is that Jesus found us lost in our junk and called us by name to follow him and live out a life of compassion, commitment, change, and celebration.

At the beginning of this chapter, we wondered why so many people who claim to be followers of Christ are living lives that don't remotely reflect the example Jesus set. Perhaps you are looking at your own life and feeling convicted. Living out the gospel Jesus intended is not easy. If it was easy,

THE GOSPEL JESUS INTENDED

everyone would do it. It requires sacrifice, it often brings persecution and rejection, but I promise you it is worth it.

Any time you make a major change or decision, it should start with prayer. As you are attempting to begin this new process of living the gospel that Jesus intended, you must start with getting on your knees before God. The Bible says that the "earnest prayer of a righteous person has great power and wonderful results."[4] My encouragement to you is to start praying through Luke 15. Ask God to reveal more of his love and passion for you, so that you will be able to have compassion for others. Tell him that you want to begin to learn how to reach the notorious sinners, tax collectors, and Pharisees who are living around you. Pray for opportunities to leave your comfort zone and go after someone who is lost.

Imagine what could happen if we really lived out the gospel as Jesus intended.

REDEFINING NOTORIOUS

My hope and prayer is that this book has helped you think differently about the gospel and given you a fresh perspective on who Jesus is, and what he expects from us. If you have been inspired or convicted to change in any way, I want to offer a challenge to you.

Whenever I am preaching, I like to ask two questions at the end of my message. The first question is:

WHAT IS GOD SAYING TO YOU?

What has God been speaking to you throughout this book? I can write a thousand more words, but it is useless unless you are listening to what the Holy Spirit is telling you about how this relates to your life.

The second question is:

WHAT ARE YOU GOING TO DO ABOUT IT?

There are broken, screwed up, spiritually dead people all around you, for whom Jesus died, but they're not just going to figure it out on their own. How can they know unless they hear about him, and how can they hear unless someone tells them?[5] The world doesn't need Christians who just sit around reading books and never put their faith into action. Are you willing to accept the challenge? Are you willing to let go of your pride, walk away from your security, or sacrifice your needs so that someone can honestly hear the good news and be changed the way I believe God is changing you?

I don't know about you, but I don't want to live a life that is forgotten, or that didn't make any difference in the world. When Jesus was on earth, he didn't just hang out with notorious sinners, he actually became notorious himself. Everywhere he went, people knew his name and what to expect. "This guy eats with sinners. He performs miracles. This guy is a prophet." I want to be notorious! Not for my own fame, but for his. I want to see the word redefined by a movement of Christ followers who are willing to risk their reputations and their lives for the sake of the gospel.

This is what Jesus intended for us.

That day I told my friend Steve about Jesus in the grocery store parking lot, my reputation began to shift. Instead of being the notorious troublemaker, I started to become known as someone who Jesus had changed. To this day, I encounter people from my past who are in shock that I am now a pastor. I am humbled that God has used me to reach thousands of people, and that this number grows every day. If God can do that with me, then I know that he can do it with you, too. I honestly believe that when we decide to accept the calling on our life to live out the gospel as Jesus intended, we can truly become

notorious.

CHAPTER ELEVEN

REFLECTION & APPLICATION

What is God saying to you?

What are you going to do about it?

Now that you've read this book, what do you want to be notorious for?

NOTES

CHAPTER 1
1. Romans 3:23.

CHAPTER 2
1. John 14:16-17.
2. "Compassion." Def.1. *The New Oxford American Dictionary Third Edition*. New York: Oxford UP, 2010. Print.
3. Romans 5:8.
4. 1 Corinthians 9:22, NIV.
5. Luke 19:10.

CHAPTER 3
1. Luke 19.
2. Exodus 20:1-17, KJV.
3. "You must not have any other god but me." Exodus 20:3.
4. Matthew 3:7; Matthew 23:26; Mark 7:6; Matthew 23:27.

CHAPTER 4
1. John 8:11.
2. Mark 2:5.
3. Matthew 4:17.
4. Matthew 4:18-22.
5. Mark 2:17, TRUTHQUEST.
6. Psalm 119:105.
7. Luke 14:35.
8. Luke 14:26.
9. John 6:53.
10. John 6:67.

CHAPTER 5
1. Luke 20:1-2.
2. Psalm 139:14, NIV.
3. Matthew 7:15-20.
4. Acts 5:39, TRUTHQUEST.
5. John 15:18-20, TRUTHQUEST.
6. Matthew 26:57-66.
7. Luke 6:29-32, TRUTHQUEST.

8. Psalm 23:5.
9. Luke 23:24.

CHAPTER 6
1. Hebrews 4:15.
2. Peatross, Fred.
3. Matthew 11:19.
4. Luke 2:46-47.
5. Luke 19:9,10.

CHAPTER 7
1. Rose, Frank. "The Art of Immersion: Why Do We Tell Stories?" *Wired.com*. N.p., 8 March 2011. Web. 14 February 2014. <http://www.wired.com/business/2011/03/why-do-we-tell-stories>.
2. Matthew 13:13-15.
3. John 16:13.

CHAPTER 8
1. Matthew 9:36, NIV.
2. Luke 15:4.
3. Luke 19:10.
4. John 10:11.
5. Isaiah 53:6, NIV.

CHAPTER 9
1. Psalm 40:4
2. Psalm 33:4

CHAPTER 10
1. Genesis 1:27.
2. 1 Corinthians 1:30; Matthew 7:11.
3. Lewis, C.S. *Mere Christianity*. New York: Macmillan, 1952.
4. Luke 9:23.
5. Romans 5:3-11.

CHAPTER 11
1. 2 Timothy 3:5.
2. Colossians 1:16.
3. Hebrews 12:2.
4. James 5:16.
5. Romans 10:14.

ACKNOWLEDGEMENTS

Stephanie: I love you very much. Thank you for standing by my side every time I want to try something crazy.

Parker James: Your Daddy didn't know he could love anyone as much as he loves you. You were my motivation for writing this book. My prayer is that the world and the church you grow up in are better than the ones I did, and that my ceiling would become your floor.

The Movement: I just love being your pastor. You guys never cease to amaze me with your generosity, your acceptance and love of others, and your belief that we can change the world from Nowhere, Ohio. The best is yet to come.

Andy Warren, Chris Gilkey, Chip Trebilcock, Konan Stephens, John Weisman, Jimn Kyles, Jeremy Foster: You men have taught me how to be a husband, a dad, and how to pastor people the way Jesus wants. I would not be the man I am today if it wasn't for you and your investment into my life. Thank you.

Andrew, Mary, Terri, Marci: Thank you for being a sounding board, for researching ideas, and helping me shape the way this book turned out. Isaac: Your design is exactly what I wanted. Please come work for me.

The Staff of The Movement: I know you all work so many hours that no one ever sees. Thank you for working as hard and as passionately as you do to carry out the vision. Thank you for making it possible for me to take time to write this book without worrying that our church might burn to the ground. You guys rock. I'm so proud to lead you.

NOTORIOUSBOOK.COM